ESSENTIAL BALANCES

STOP LOOKING AND START SEEING WHAT MAKES ORGANIZATIONS WORK

IVO VELITCHKOV

Edited by
ROB WORTH

KVISTGAARD

First edition

Ebook ISBN 978-1-8383386-0-2

Paperback ISBN 978-1-8383386-1-9

Published by: Kvistgaard

Cover design by Sylvia Atipova

Edited by Rob Worth, WorthEditing.com

ESSENTIAL BALANCES

CONTENTS

FOREWORD

by Luc Hoebeke

THE WORD "SIMPLIFY" has two contradictory meanings. The first, reducing complexity by eliminating relevant issues, is what leads to reductionism, one of the characteristics of the classical "scientific" disciplinary approach. While the second, integrating complicated issues into a more unifying whole, is a more difficult way to deal with real-world complexity.

This book is of the second kind. It embodies simplicity by focusing on essential balances in organizations, and the depth becomes visible once one starts to go through the notes after each chapter. The notes refer to authors, such as Spencer-Brown, Stafford Beer, Varela, Glanville, Luhmann, and others, who have also been influential upon my career as a reflective practitioner. They are not easy reading, except for those who recognize their value in making sense of a practitioner's complex relationship with the always undecidable dilemmas he or she is confronted with in organizational life.

The stories in the chapters, which at first glance are easy

reading, stress an important perspective for understanding organizations: balance as opposed to equilibrium. Balance and tension are two sides of the same medal: when marching on our two feet, or riding a bike, we continuously put ourselves out of equilibrium, nearly falling but then keeping our balance. But sometimes we lose our balance and fall down on the ground. Nevertheless, we restart our balancing act, the only way to make us go further.

A balancing act deals with contradictions, never getting it right. This is in contrast to the simplistic algorithmic worldview, which looks for optima, win–win situations, best practices, and other problem-solving approaches.

The three balances Ivo develops in his book, Autonomy and Cohesion, Stability and Diversity, and Exploration and Exploitation, will be recognized by most of those who are not running away from tensions, conflicts, and contradictions in the way they work in organizations. Tensions, conflicts and contradictions, which are mostly seen as "bad" things, in fact, form the "tonus" of organizational life, and keep them out of the dead end of equilibria.

The last two chapters, Stimuli and Responses, and Productive Paradoxes, conceptually deepen the worldview behind the chapters about the essential balances. They stress where in the organization the balances manifest themselves: on its boundaries. It is on the margins, on the periphery of systems, where practitioners following Ivo's perspective should put their focus and efforts to understand organizational dynamics. Where people in the organization are confronted with material reality, with the "other" ones, is where balancing acts are needed. Most boardrooms look alike and are places of equilibrium. That is why people in them fall asleep with a false sense of controlling the "events", having their finger on the "pulse" through Excel charts, reports, scoreboards, data-mining results, and other virtual gimmicks, mostly copying what they hear other boardrooms are busy with, and helped by "boardroom" consultants.

What is marginal or peripheral, is not attractive, because it always has some chaotic character. Complexity is too often perceived as chaos! How easy is the "helicopter view", which mostly only lets us see a cloud landscape? Boardrooms are often situated on the highest floor of the head office! And all cloud landscapes look similar.

Ivo's book will help everyone who is concerned and loves organizational life to look where it is relevant. The contradictions and conflicts cannot be dealt with in a relevant way when there is no insight into the boundaries, which can emerge anywhere, even in the boardroom.

Everything human beings are doing, is done on a human scale. Recognizing the essential balances in every human-scale environment, on the shop floor, over the counter, and in the boardroom, may become a powerful habit for dealing with the unpredictability, the undecidability, and the complexity that human beings discovered can be dealt with by organizations and organizational life. This also requires simplicity, in the sense of humility. Understanding that each person in the organization has his or her idiosyncratic way of looking at organizational life, and trying to make sense of the conflicts and contradictions in a joint accommodation effort, is the way to resilience and balance, in short, to a fascinating life.

If we have a universe, which is improbable although it exists, it is because the Second Law of Thermodynamics has two forms. One is concerned with the pressure to even out energy: that is the form which belongs to our stereotyped conception of the universe. It betokens death. The other form is about information content, which leads to greater organization and increasing complexity. That form betokens life.

We should not regard these principles as contraries. We should not think the Second Law of Thermodynamics as warring with some perverse other law. These are forms of the same principle, which between them express the balance of nature.

— Stafford Beer, *Platform for Change*

INTRODUCTION

In the late 1990s, I managed a software company for five years and stayed on the board for five more. The company started small, then grew, but not enough to match its ambitions. That's why for all large tenders it had to partner with a well-established, international company, usually one of the big consultancies. This meant that our work had to be organized and delivered according to the respective prime contractor's frameworks and methodologies. These prescriptions guided the way the change was implemented in the client organization.

It was fascinating and useful for me to learn so many different methodologies, even when they imposed restrictions that slowed down the actual service delivery. They all had some good bits and some limitations. The deficiencies I discovered inspired me later on, when I became a freelance consultant, to start creating my own frameworks, models, and methodologies. Yet, in the following years, I learned that no matter how good, scalable, or flexible such approaches may be, organizations are way too complex and their environment much too unpredictable to rely on prescriptions.

Organizations can't even rely on performance indicators, no matter how advanced we became in managing data.

Going beyond prescriptions and metrics was challenging but rewarding. What turned out to be even more difficult was to find a simple and clear way to share what I learned. I started doing it through workshops and now, after much honing, refining, and feedback, and in more detail, I've tried to do it with this book.

This book is about what makes organizations work, what it takes to see when they don't work, and how to ensure they do when the environment is complex and unpredictable.

This book is also about balances.

When our meal is not tasty, we add salt. Just enough. If we add too much, it's not tasty again – but in a different way. We maintain these kinds of balances with ease, and without thinking, in our daily lives, but we are not so good at seeing and maintaining balances in our organizations. This book is about acquiring that skill.

Why is this important?

We depend on organizations and on how they are organized. People spend most of their lives working in and with organizations. We are coupled with organizations. So everyone is happier if our organizations work well. And for some, it is their daily job to ensure that.

To be coupled with organizations means that we are mutually dependent and we co-adapt. But humans and organizations have had different starts on this planet. We humans have been around for millions of years. Organizations are much younger. They started appearing just a few centuries ago. No wonder that while in society we advanced to the level of democracy, most big organizations have only reached the stage of feudalism.

Indeed, what we call *organization* is young. But if we look not just at those that *are* organizations, but more broadly at things that *have* organization, we can accelerate our learning. And there is good and bad news.

It turns out, things that maintain their own organization have common ways to deal with environmental challenges. The good news is that we can learn from millions of years of evolution. But how can we grasp so much and access it in a way that's useful and usable? What I find fundamental, and yet largely ignored, are three essential balances. They are common for organisms and for organizations, and they don't depend on size or whether organizations are hierarchical or flat. New business models and new ways of working don't change the importance of these balances. That's also good news.

The bad news is that although the balances are common and only three are essential, there are infinite ways to maintain them. Retrospectively, we can find what worked, but we cannot prescribe it. We cannot extract best practices and develop methodologies. We can instead train our eye to see patterns and recognize trends before they become big problems.

But organizations can go out of balance in ways not experienced before. Then it is equally important to work on thinking habits and skills that we'll need to invent new ways of restoring the balance.

Organizing

To deal with complexity, we organize. Organizing is powerful since it can both split and join. We break down what's coming to us into pieces to make sense of it (split). But to handle the pieces, we group them by similarities (join). Then we distribute what comes next to one of these groups (split). When all that is too much for us to handle alone, we get together and create organizations (join). Then we categorize what's coming to our organizations into different types of problems (split). Each problem needs work. We subdivide the organizations into as many divisions as there are types of problems so that each division can take care of one or a few problems (split). But our divisions still need to work together (join). When there are many divisions, and since they need to coordinate their actions, the internal complexity increases. The organization is our new world now, and it is complex by our own doing. We must keep organizing and reorganizing to deal with it.

Deal originates from *divide*. It initially meant only *to distribute*. Now it also means *to cope, manage,* and *control*. Yet it seems that we remained faithful to the original meaning. We manage things by dividing them. We eat an elephant piece by piece, we start a journey of a thousand miles with a single step, and we divide to conquer.

Meanwhile, we need to translate the unknown into the known. To do that, we devise classes of things (those groupings made by…) and criteria (…similarities) for classification. We know the current members of the classes and we know the rules to apply to something that is unknown so we can classify it. We deal the external stimuli (this time in the initial sense – without *with*), like a deck of cards, into the boxes we have devised, based on the properties the stimuli appear to have. Unlike real card players, these boxes cannot think.

But we can't deal with bigger things on our own. We do things together, and if that works better, an organization emerges. It starts a life of its own and, together with us, it takes care of itself. The initial reason to be: "if that works better", is quickly forgotten. This is not surprising, as the environment doesn't sleep and throws us new challenges. To manage them, we now split ourselves into groups – new kinds of boxes. We classify the new problems and we put them into our new boxes. The new boxes, however, *can* think. They *are* like real card players. We call these small organizations within the organization, teams, units, and departments, and they all live a life of their own too. The new boxes get better at what they do and at handling threats and opportunities. Some gain power and begin to choose their cards themselves.

Occasionally a new card comes that doesn't fit an existing type. Then we adapt our model. We create a new group to handle this new type of problem. The organization gets more complex. The new problem is taken care of, at least on the surface. Yet sometimes, this kind of response doesn't work at all. To split as a choice (to analyze and classify), or the particular way of splitting (method for analyzing or classification), or the assignment (who is made responsible), does not produce the expected results. The new card that is dealt comes from an unfamiliar deck. It is bigger and refuses to get smaller. Being bigger doesn't always make it easier to see. It might go unnoticed for a long time.

How can we deal with these stubborn cards? Sooner or later, the groups we split into are pressed to work together to handle these big cards. We respond by devising methods and technologies for coordination. In turn, the coordination methods take up resources, and at some point, they start to live a life of their own as well. We end up having different types of organizations within the organization, some for the core work, some for coordination.

Organizations are everywhere and some are so familiar it is easy to forget how much of our lives depend on them. We work for and live in and with organizations. Anything we do with others is some form of organization, from the scout pack to the tennis club, from the political demonstration to the kickaround in the park on a Sunday afternoon. Most of the products and services we use are produced and provided by companies. We are citizens of states and we participate in organizations as employees, members, managers, owners, or consultants. Our own families, in our house and connected down the street or across the globe, are organizations. Our health and the quality of our lives depend on organizations. On what they do and how they do it. On their performance and work environment. That's why we are interested in having organizations that are healthy and functional. But how can we tell if they are or not?

Measuring

Traditionally, we judge organizations the same way we would an athlete: we measure. We measure the time an athlete takes to run 100 metres to rate her performance. In a similar way, we measure sales, client satisfaction, and cost of services in our organizations.

As the importance of performance measurement grew, we learned that these post-factum measures are not enough. They tell us too late that something is wrong. We started calling them "lagging indicators". Our attention then shifted to live measures: "leading indicators". With this grew the interest in studying business processes to spot a bad trend in time so we can take action before it's too late. That worked up to a point, but only for routine, well-structured processes. Now we have fewer of those and more unstructured, knowledge-driven processes. It's increasingly difficult to measure them, as each time a process is run, it is different. And how reliable is performance measurement anyway? We can rely on performance indicators when measuring a machine's or even an athlete's performance. But they are much less reliable with organizations. Why?

First, more than a century ago, quantum mechanics showed how measuring influences the measured. We successfully ignored this when creating new technologies. Then we thought we could also ignore it when measuring organizations. We expect organizations to be rational and work like machines. But they are not, and they don't.

Second, we turn some measures into targets for people to achieve. But people are adaptive, and they find their own way to hit their targets. And often, it's not the way those who devised the measures had in mind.

Third, we trust objective measures to understand subjective phenomena. Take the weather, for example. When I want to go out, I check the forecast. I'm interested in the temperature, but that's only because I believe it will tell me if it is going to be cold or hot, or rather, if I will feel it as cold or hot. The difference made the forecast services also give a "feels-like" temperature, which accounts for humidity, cloud cover, wind, sun intensity and angle. It's an attempt to overcome the shortcomings of the objective measure with a measure of objective subjectivity. Definitely an improvement. Yet, if I've spent the last six months in a warmer climate, my feels-like temperature will be lower than that of people who stayed in the local climate. And if I haven't been anywhere, but just haven't slept well, I'll also feel colder. Even the colour of the houses when I go out in the morning may influence my perception of warmth. The feels-like forecast, no matter how good, will never know how it feels like really, as it can't know the history, the context, and the condition of those who *can* feel.

One way or another, organizations can learn how well they perform, and they can learn to perform better. But often organizations function below their potential. Consider our athlete. She can't run fast today as she doesn't feel well. How can we find out what's wrong? We might do a blood test, and any results that are outside norms will prompt further investigation of the problem. But that's difficult to apply for organizations. Measuring their performance is already challenging. Diagnosing them is even harder.

That's one of the objectives of this book. It will show a way of looking at organizations to help diagnose them.

Organizing uses the power of opposing forces, like separating and integrating (split and join), and it is successful when it balances them. Indicators of a blood test must be within a healthy range. Similarly, certain balances need to be maintained in organizations.

Prescribing

Once we are able to diagnose organizations, we need to learn how to heal them – or better – to teach them the habits of healthy living.

How do we traditionally go about it?

We look at successful organizations, analyze their practices, check what's common, generalize, and try to copy. In other words, we create and use best practices, methodologies, and frameworks. Currently, there are many such tools. I know, because as I mentioned at the beginning, I used a lot and developed a few. The big consulting companies, and especially those that advise on management and IT, thrive on them. Consultancies recruit bright young people, train them to apply some proprietary or adopted methodologies, and then deploy their new consultants in the field to diagnose, advise, fix, and implement. But these young consultants are smarter than their tools. Soon they learn what works and what doesn't. The former novices become too experienced to be wasted as individual consultants and get promoted, which means they are simultaneously pushed forward and pulled backward. They are pushed forward as speakers and negotiators so they can attract and win new business, and they are pulled backward as managers to steer the time-selling machine, oiled with good methodologies. This model makes methodologies and best practices in high demand, so the old ones get improved, and new ones are being produced at a high rate.

The first thing I realized when using methodologies is that there is no methodology that can guarantee success and not using any does not guarantee failure. I learned later that the adoption of a methodology or a practice comes along with a lot of hidden adaptations or productive misinterpretations. The success of most methodologies owes more to the adaptive capabilities of their adopters than to the qualities of the methodologies.

Methodologies and best practices may be very different, but they all have one thing in common: they are prescriptive.

Some best practices are very useful. In fact, most mature and well-applied best practices for carrying out some technical task, from taking a blood test, painting a wall, or repairing an engine, to building a factory or a ship, are indeed valuable (as long as they don't suffocate innovation). Best practices are also valuable in training because that's a controlled environment. They can help a sports team prepare for a match, but won't help *during* the match. They are even less useful in organizations where the rules of the game change. Why is that? In short, best practices are based on correlations, oversimplification, and ignorance. Worst of all, they create bad habits. We'll unpack these in turn.

How do best practices come about? Certain organizations become known as successful according to some norms. Let's call these organizations "best-practice pioneers". They become known because they are given exposure by the media or by the actions of "best-practice discoverers". The best-practice discoverer studies the pioneers to find out what made them successful. The discoverer first takes certain effects, identifies commonalities, and selects what they believe were the causes of success. The commonalities are then generalized and embellished. From that moment, they begin their life as prescriptions. These prescriptions come packaged and labelled. Later they are tested, and then, based on feedback, reappear in more mature forms and variations. In some cases, they're supplied with scalability criteria and conditions for successful application. The successes and failures of those that apply them give birth to best practices on applying best practices.

The first problem comes from the selection of patterns. The best-practice discoverers point to common patterns among best-practice pioneers. These common patterns are thought to be the reason for success by virtue of being … common. That is, of course, the well-known problem of correlation. But it's more interesting than that.

There are three intertwined issues. The first is the selection of what to pay attention to and what to ignore. It's arbitrary and full of assumptions. The same holds for the second issue, which is the choice of the relations that are deemed to have caused success. Doing that, led to this. These relations guide the discoverer's attention, and that brings the third issue: every pattern that supports the hypothesis based on the selected commonalities is preferred over those that don't. Thus, the selections, the correlation, and the confirmation bias support each other, ending up with a coherent and convincing story. The discoverer is then joined by other people and organizations. They confirm the discovered patterns, often refining and extending them with their own findings.

Then the attention shifts to successful adopters. This comes with its own set of problems. For example, when an organization is known as a good example of adopting a certain methodology, this is done only by referencing the decision to adopt. Little attention is paid to the actual implementation, which often includes not only modifications of the methodology but also regretting making that decision.

The next problem is caused by oversimplification. We deal with things by classifying them. Classification is very important for all prescriptive methods. We can only apply methodologies to already predefined classes and we use methodologies to determine what is what. Here is the risk of oversimplification. We have our classes of things (or types and categories), and we deal with external stimuli by trying to fit them into those classes. Sometimes we force them until they do, often too busy to notice that they don't. In other words, best practices are tools for reducing the diversity of external stimuli, which is often achieved by being insensitive to them. But the insensitivity goes further.

Methodologies and best practices cannot know the context and the history of the adopting organization. Maybe they don't need to if the environment is predictable. But this is increasingly rare. Which brings another interesting phenomenon: the less predictable the world is, the higher the demand for new and better ways to deal with new problems and the shorter the time to productize methodologies and practices. As a result, methodologies and best practices adapt and proliferate. They come with better marketing and with more authority in a world in which they are less and less applicable, a world in which what has been cannot prepare you for what will come.

The worst thing is when people hide behind the authority of best practices or their proponents. Best practices create the habit of looking for best practices first, instead of thinking first.

Best practices also make people pay more attention to the average than to the outliers. But one can drown in a river that's one inch deep on average. Or think of a bar with 50 people where the average wealth of those people is 1,000. Next door is a bar with another 50 people who have an average wealth of 100,000. Two quite different sets of clientele. Then a billionaire pops into the first bar for a drink. Now the average wealth in that bar is just over 19.6 million. The billionaire finishes her banana daiquiri and goes next door – remember in this bar the average wealth is 100,000. What effect does the billionaire have on the average here? Well, it goes from 100,000 to 19.7 million. We have two bars with very different distributions of the wealth of the patrons, but the billionaire's arrival makes them seem almost the same if you just look at the average wealth after she arrives. This average of nearly 20 million tells you nothing about the distribution of wealth in either of the two bars when a billionaire is there, in the same way that per capita GDP tells you nothing about the distribution of wealth in a country. Averages don't account for outliers very well. The Earth itself is an outlier – the average planet has no life on it.

Lastly, there is the damage of the associated alternative cost: the more time people spend on learning best practices, the less time they have for training their senses to detect weak signals and for developing their capabilities for novel responses.

Glasses and habits instead

This book tries to avoid prescriptions and advice. It doesn't tell you what to do. It simply shows another way of looking at organizations.

Once you see them in this new way, the chances are you will be better equipped to understand what's actually going on. You will be able to figure out what needs to be done on your own without following prescriptions. And you will do all this adaptively, after a series of adjustments, big and small.

This is a book for working on new habits and for cultivating the habit of being conscious about the dual nature of habits. They are both enabling and constraining. As you create them, they influence the way you create them. Importantly, this book will not claim that "this is how things are". The claim is that "it is useful to create certain observational habits". More specifically, to create the habits of observation using different pairs of glasses.

"Different" implies two things. Firstly, that you are always wearing some pair of glasses, regardless of whether you realize it or not. Secondly, using new pairs of glasses is just as important as creating the habit of changing the glasses you are wearing from time to time.

I prefer "glasses" to "lens" as a metaphor here.

Of course, glasses have lenses and lenses are meant to improve vision or, at any rate, they change it. Quite often, the glasses you'll find in this book bring surprises. Where you trust your intuition, you might see things that are counterintuitive. Where you'd rather use logic, they might appear illogical. It's not intentional. It just often happens to be the case.

The first reason I prefer to talk about glasses, rather than just lenses, is that glasses have frames. The frames serve as a constant reminder that every perspective has limitations, creates a bias, and leaves a blind spot. Using the same glasses might be problematic in some situations, or in all situations if you wear them for too long. Secondly, glasses are made to fit; they are something designed for our bodies. They wouldn't fit a mouse or even another person.

So, we have thinking and acting habits to work on. The way to approach it is by using glasses. Moreover, these are glasses that you rent rather than buy or – if willing to devote the effort – grow rather than build. There are three main pairs of such glasses to see organizations through.

But what do we usually see when we look at organizations? Some see people; others see departments, organizational charts, balance sheets, profit-and-loss accounts, shares, activities, processes, products, services, capabilities, culture, information flows, knowledge, documents, operations, projects, programmes, and information systems. And why do they see these things? And more importantly: are they really there? People see them only because somebody at some point made certain distinctions, created concepts, and agreed on ways to distinguish them from what they are not. Then others found that convincing or useful. They joined, confirmed, extended, and gave life to these distinctions in language and communications. This made it possible to use them – the things organizations are believed to be made of – to evaluate, design, decide, make rules for, change, and fight for and against.

At some point, what was important was the division of labour. When the limits of such functional fragmentation became evident, the vertical and static descriptions and management of organizations were extended with horizontal and dynamic descriptions. What was distinguished then were the business processes. This went in parallel and was mutually influenced by the tendency to move from a self-centred perspective to a client-focused one. The client-focused, or so-called "inside-out" perspective, had its own deficiencies, and in some companies it evolved into "outside-in" as an attempt to better understand how customers experience the services provided by the organization. In parallel, some did not pay attention to the value chain or customer experience but more to self-regulation of different subsystems within organizations. For them, organizations were made of systems and information flows.

These sketches do not cover all views, nor do they show an evolution – the maturity states they depict coexist today. The point is that these are concepts created by people, who made a series of distinctions where other distinctions were also possible.

Using the three pairs of glasses is again a matter of distinctions, but not on what the organizations are made of. Instead, it will be about seeing relationships and how they change in different contexts, and what the impact of those changes is on the health and performance of the organizations. With these glasses, you'll start seeing certain balances.

The Three Essential Balances

There are three Essential Balances: Autonomy–Cohesion, Stability–Diversity, and Exploration–Exploitation.

Autonomy and Cohesion

If there is not enough autonomy in an organization, it will not be effective, it will not adapt quickly, and it won't be resilient. But if there is no cohesion, the organization will not be efficient. It will grow silos. They will pursue their own continuation and growth at the expense of the organization.

Autonomy and cohesion need to be balanced at various levels. As "level" is a spatial metaphor, it implies hierarchy. That's not the intention, and hierarchy is only a special case. These levels are not arbitrary. Each level refers to a different scale of organizational identity. That's why the balance between autonomy and cohesion (and the other two balances) works in both hierarchical and non-hierarchical organizations. They do it in different ways, but once you have the habit of using the glasses, you'll be able to see how they do it and when they don't. You'll be able to see that things that seem different, such as meetings, mottos, complaining about the weather, rules, and language, actually play the same role in the context of the balance.

All organizations need autonomy for their immediate effectiveness and long-term viability. By "all", I also mean the organizations within an organization: teams, projects, programmes, units, departments, and subsidiaries. At the same time, there should be cohesion so that the organization does not disintegrate, so that it conserves energy by not duplicating efforts, by economies of scale, and by synergies. The focus will be on the organization, but the importance of that balance does not stop at the personal or organizational level.

Beyond the organizational level, autonomy is exercised as freedom of market initiative and action, and cohesion is manifested as market coordination and regulation. Various ecosystems maintain this balance. Sometimes autonomy and cohesion even enable each other. For example, the World Wide Web provides the autonomy to share and get information. This is enabled by the cohesion from using the same standards for network protocols and markup languages.

Autonomy is needed at the personal level for individual action. The more freedom there is to choose how to do what needs to be done, the higher the chance it will be done well. Autonomy is balanced by cohesion forces. Some of them originate from the individual, such as the need to belong to a social group or to maximize self-esteem. Others originate from the team, which has its own cohesion concern. The cohesion forces work not only between people but also within individuals. One example of such a force is what we commonly refer to as personal integrity; another comes from the personal ability to deal with multiple tasks that are competing for time. Habits, emotions, and social identities are cohesion forces too.

Stability and Diversity

The second balance is that of stability and diversity. It can be seen as three balances, one for stability, one for diversity, and one where they depend on each other.

Stability in organizations is dynamic, yet viable organizations have the ability to maintain it and to re-establish it when it is disturbed. When valuable people leave, others are recruited. When market share shrinks, new services are added, or new markets are explored. When a competitor uses and benefits from a new technology, it is adopted, or a better one is found.

Occasionally, organizations are disturbed in a way not experienced before. Then, stability can only be restored using novel means. If what has been tried hasn't solved the problem, there will still be many more choices that haven't been tried. No matter how much we think we can predict, we can never know which will work. Hence the need for diversity. It could be a different kind of diversity – people, ideas, or experiments.

Stability is not always a good thing, and neither is too much diversity. Organizations enjoying long periods of stability tend to develop organizational atrophy, hyper-efficiency, and blindness. Their ability to respond to changes is toned down, as well as their innovation capability and market sensitivity. At the same time, too much diversity can cause an unhealthy level of internal conflict and complexity.

Exploration and Exploitation

The third balance between exploration and exploitation is, at first glance, a resource allocation problem. Should you exploit a resource, refine a technology, and extend the offering to existing clients? Or should you look for alternative resources, new technologies, and explore new markets? It is equally a viability problem. An animal needs to eat (exploit) to have the energy to look for more food (explore). A company needs a flow of resources now, so that it can finance research and innovation to ensure its viability in the future.

Organizations tend to over-exploit and under-explore. Why? Because the expected results from exploitation are usually known, while the potential results from exploration are always unknown. There is certainty and immediate return from exploitation. Exploration is prone to fail and difficult to defend. That's why it needs more attention.

The three balances are related. Exploration requires more autonomy and diversity. Exploitation can be achieved when there is coherence and stability.

Growing the habit of seeing these three balances in completely different situations and at various scales is useful on its own. But it gets even more compelling when they are combined or when you use one pair of glasses to look at yourself looking at something using another pair of glasses. This ability is further enhanced by the generic balance between *stimuli* and *responses.*

At the end, there is an extra pair of glasses, through which organizations look like a network of paradoxical decisions.

Who is this book for?

The balances described in the following chapters are essential at the individual, organizational, and societal levels. The focus of this book is on the organizational level. Even so, there will be plenty of examples for the other two. Learning to see the balances at the individual level is important for maintaining the habit, as we have ourselves handy at all times. Seeing the balances at the societal level also contributes to honing the skill, for some phenomena are more visible there than at the organizational level.

Since the balances work at all three levels, this book might be useful for everyone. But as the focus is on organizations, it is more valuable to those of you who work in, or with, organizations. For example, if you are an individual artist, general practitioner, or a sole trader, it might not be as useful to you as if you are a manager, consultant, or entrepreneur.

Here is a list of roles for whom this book should be of the highest value:

- Managers at any level, from team leaders to CEOs
- Human Resource managers
- Change Agents
- Governance professionals
- Enterprise Architects
- Project managers
- Business analysts
- Organizational Consultants
- Coaches
- Business process optimization experts
- Policy officers in the Public Sector
- Boards of directors
- Strategy advisers
- Entrepreneurs

How is this book written?

Although there are no diagrams in this book, there are stories. And while there is no indication of notes in the text, you'll find plenty of notes after each chapter. These decisions deserve an explanation.

About Notes

The text of this book is full of references and statements which need elaboration. There are plenty of good ways to deal with them: showing citation references, footnotes, endnotes, and elaborations in text boxes. On one hand, not referring to the sources of ideas is not an option; credit should go where it's due. And knowing the sources will help the most curious of you when searching for answers that are implied in this book but not elaborated on. On the other hand, indications of references are interruptions. Sometimes it might be interesting for the reader to stop and check the reference, but that comes at the risk of breaking the flow. My attempt to strike a balance here comes to the following solution.

You'll find no indications of references, footnotes, elaborations, or citations in the text. This is to avoid interruptions and distractions. After each chapter, there are notes. These notes start with the part of the text that needs a reference or elaboration. This excerpt is in bold. It is then followed by an explanation that often includes citations and references to the sources, which you can find at the end of the book.

Notes don't serve only to elaborate, clarify, and point to references. They also serve to balance. When a certain perspective is chosen in the main text, it's not always helpful to nuance it there as it may unnecessarily complicate matters and blur the main point. That role is left to the notes.

All concepts within the book are explained avoiding technical jargon as much as possible. The notes are free from that constraint.

There, you may find unfamiliar concepts. Even when they are briefly explained in the notes, if you are interested to learn more, you may need to study the referenced sources.

Not making reference indications in the main text indicates that if you are not interested in further details, or don't have time at the moment, or for any other reason, it's safe to read the main text only and skip all the notes.

Stories

The only "interruption" of the flow of the text are a few stories. Some of them are fictional or semi-fictional (made out of common patterns of real cases). Others provide a short explanation of a certain phenomenon, for example, how the immune system works. Those explanations are based on a chosen theory, where another choice was also possible. The important thing is that for the purpose of this book, they serve the same role as the fictional stories. And even if the difference between the two is blurred, that's fine. In any case, the text after the stories provides analysis and elaboration. Some parts of the stories are referred to in other chapters, or it could be the same part already discussed but looked at and explained in a different way. And there might be parts of the stories left untouched and open to your interpretation. Similar considerations support the decision not to have any diagrams and tables in the text.

No Diagrams

I have produced a lot of models, many of which had graphical renditions. Yet, I decided neither to reuse any of those, nor to produce new ones here. Why?

First, because of the risk of oversimplification, mentioned earlier.

Second, I believe that the best model of an organization is the organization itself. Organizations are complex, while their models are simple. No wonder people are attracted to using models to help make sense of organizations. As this is a book for creating new habits, it also has the ambition to start creating the habit of using the organization as a model of itself, and using the sets of glasses offered is a good first step.

Third, the dominant notion that our cognition works by creating representations in our heads is giving way to a much more coherent understanding where representations play no role. Simply put, the way we learn to ride a bicycle does not involve having a model of a bicycle in our heads. While mental models may turn out to be a myth, the physical and informational models are valuable as something we create and interact with. But that practice stabilizes its own set of habits, and this book is about a different one.

The fourth reason is related to accessibility concerns and the option to fully experience this content in an audiobook.

And fifth, although diagrams can provide clarity, and it may be true that some pictures are worth more than a thousand words, pictures also fix the possible interpretations. Reading is a process of co-creation. Your interaction with the text will produce a variety of images which I can't imagine. I find that diversity too valuable to reduce it with a few diagrams. Hence, I'll reserve those for seminars and workshops.

This book has been a struggle to find its own essential balances. The main one is the balance between *useful* and *used*. I'm trying from one side, not to oversimplify things, so that what I provide is *useful*, but it shouldn't also be overwhelming, so that it is actually *used*.

NOTES

1. *Deal* originates from *divide*. It initially meant only *to distribute*.

> *From Old English* dæl *"part, share, quantity, amount," from Proto-Germanic* *dailaz *(source also of Old Norse* deild, *Old Frisian* del, *Dutch* deel, *Old High German and German* teil, *Gothic* dails *"part, share"), from PIE* *dail- *"to divide" (source also of Old Church Slavonic* delu *"part," Lithuanian* dalis*). Business sense of "transaction, bargain" is 1837, originally slang.* (Harper, 2018)

The original word kept its meaning in modern Dutch, *delen*, "divide, separate into parts", first-person *deel*; and also meaning "part" as a noun; as well as in Swedish *dela*, and in some Slavic languages, for example, делить [*delít'*] in Russian.

2. Meanwhile, we need to translate the unknown into the known.

According to Luhmann, organizations are made up of a network of decisions, the main function of which is uncertainty absorption.

> *Organizations operate in a world they cannot know. This world is transformed through uncertainty absorption into a known world; it is replaced by a known world. This requires in retrospect a first decision, which inscribes a distinction into the world, for example, by defining a purpose.* (Seidl, Becker, & Luhmann, 2005)

This is another perspective and a more general way of looking at organizations as absorbers of complexity. Before Luhmann, in a similar way, Stafford Beer (Beer, 1980) applied Ashby's Law of Requisite Variety (Ashby, 2015 [1956]). Luhmann's perspective will be presented in "Productive Paradoxes". The variety absorption perspective is the main topic of the "Stimuli and Responses" chapter.

3. [W]e turn some measures into targets for people to achieve. But people are adaptive, and they find their own way to hit their targets.

Marylin Strathern, in Strathern (1997), paraphrases Goodhart's law to:

> *When a measure becomes a target, it ceases to be a good measure.*

The original formulation by Charles Goodhart (Goodhart, 1984) is:

Any observed statistical regularity will tend to collapse once pressure is placed upon it for control purposes.

And this is not something specific to performance measurement. Risk assessment suffers from similar deficiencies (Taleb, 2018).

4. [W]e trust objective measures to understand subjective phenomena.

In most of the projects I managed or was in a good position to observe, there was little relationship between project performance indicators and client satisfaction. Some were considered as a failure by the client when the project finished, and rightly so. Then years later, the same project was remembered by the same people as successful. Often, it was because these people had gathered maturity in the meantime and were able to assess it differently. In other cases, a project either hit targets but was still considered to have failed or didn't and yet was celebrated as a success. To understand this, I started using something I called the "4U Test". The implied "for you" was intended, but the four U's (two U's and one W) came from the following questions: "Does it work?", "Is it used?", and "Is it useful?" In most cases, if a positive answer to all three questions stabilized for some period after the project, the satisfaction of the client was stable as well. And yet, it didn't always work. This led to my interest in studying organizational paradoxes, which are described in the last chapter of this book.

5. Consultancies recruit bright young people, train them to apply some proprietary or adopted methodologies, and then deploy their new consultants in the field to diagnose, advise, fix, and implement.

Recruiting bright young people does not only work because it's efficient and predictable due to the application of methodologies and best practices. Young people believe in what works, but don't have enough experience to know what doesn't. Instead of being a drawback, their lack of experience complements the organizational "forgetfulness", which, according to Brunsson, is one of the drivers of organizational reforms. The reform in turn creates a constant need for more management consulting services.

> *[O]rganizational reforms are driven by problems to be addressed, by solutions to be applied, and by forgetfulness. The greater the supply of any of these factors, the more likely it is that reforms will occur. Without problems, reforms are difficult to justify; without solutions they cannot be formulated; and without forgetfulness there is a risk that people will be discouraged by the fact that similar reforms have been tried and have failed in the past.* (Brunsson, 2009)

Now, what is forgotten will be kept as such if the reform is justified as something never attempted before, as believed by the young consultants.

> *Forgetfulness can be promoted by the use of consultants with limited experience of the implementation and long-term effects of reforms.* (ibid.)

6. The success of most methodologies owes more to the adaptive capabilities of their adopters than to the qualities of the methodologies.

Organizations are closed self-referential systems and they cannot receive direct input from another organization (Luhmann, 1995). When they adopt a methodology or best practice, they always reconstruct its meaning according to their internal logic.

> *The resulting reconstruction necessarily differs from the original, although the underlying label (e.g., 'Balanced Scorecard', 'FiveForces') may still be the same.* (Rasche & Seidl, 2017)

7. Little attention is paid to the actual implementation, which often includes not only modifications of the methodology but also regretting making that decision.

According to Brunsson, the modern situation favours localization over generalization. What is general is transferable and what is particular is dismissed as an exception. That is maintained by the organizational hope that keeps the standards "on an attractively abstract level without being compromised by the complications of the everyday world" (Brunsson, 2009). It's again this hope which helps to downplay the importance of implementational problems:

> *When looking at others who have embraced a standard, hope makes it relevant to learn from their decisions – not necessarily from their practice. And implementation problems in one's own organization do not immediately (if ever) give rise to the conclusion that the standards promoted by a reform are wrong, and therefore unworthy of recommending to others.* (ibid.)

8. [P]er capita GDP tells you nothing about the distribution of wealth in a country.

Thinking in terms of averages and "per capita" is a manifestation of linear thinking. But biological and social system scale non-linearly. For organisms, the bigger the size, the slower the metabolic rate – there is economy of scale. Organizations and cities also need less energy the bigger they are, but due to positive feedback, there are other metrics which scale super-linearly. For example, the bigger the city, the bigger the salaries, more innovations, but also more crime and spread of diseases (West, 2017).

9. Moreover, these are glasses that you rent rather than buy or – if willing to devote the effort – grow rather than build.

First, I'm addressing the risk of attachment. Once you buy an idea, it can open a lot of new paths and opportunities. But it can also obscure your vision and preclude other opportunities. A thing you learn and turn into a belief can sometimes be the biggest obstacle to learn something else potentially more valuable.

Instead of buying ideas (packaged here as glasses for seeing balances), it is better to just rent them. Not like renting a house, more like renting a car. With that car, you can go somewhere, stay there, or go further, or elsewhere. If it is unsuitable for a particular road or destination, you can go back and rent another car.

But if you are convinced of the value of these "glasses", then when investing, it's important to understand their nature from the outset. In such an investment, you should be more of a gardener than a builder. These glasses are like flowers. They need soil, water, sun, and care. They are alive and when they grow, they might not look the way you initially imagined them to.

10. People see them only because somebody at some point made certain distinctions, created concepts, and agreed on ways to distinguish them from what they are not.

For more details on distinctions, see Velitchkov (2015).

11. When the limits of such functional fragmentation became evident, the vertical and static descriptions and management of organizations were extended with horizontal and dynamic descriptions.

We describe organizations from different perspectives, based on different concerns (International Organization for Standardization, 2011). For some, the organization structure is in focus, for others, processes. An organization can be described as a group of capabilities or services, or as having a particular culture. Some descriptions need only one element – decisions (such a perspective is provided in the last chapter, "Productive Paradoxes"). Others require roles, functions, processes, services, products, technical infrastructure, rules, and documents. When using the glasses of the essential balances, the answer to the question, "what is an organization made of?" is simple: organizations.

12. [T]he dominant notion that our cognition works by creating representations in our heads is giving way to a much more coherent understanding where representations play no role.

Cognitivism, the first school in Cognitive Science, which appeared in the 1950s, sees cognition as mental processing of symbols that represent features of the world. The next school, Connectionism, which originated during the 1980s, sees representation as corresponding not to symbols, but to the global state of the neural network. Yet, the idea that the cognition works through representations was kept. This notion was first challenged by the Enactive school of Cognitive Science, showing that:

> *cognition is not the representation of a pregiven world by a pregiven mind but rather the enactment of a world and mind on the basis of a history of the variety of actions that a being in the world performs.* (Varela, Thompson, & Rosch, 1992)

1

AUTONOMY AND COHESION

Autonomy means, literally, self-law. To see what this entails, it is easier to contrast it with its mirror image, allomony or external law. This is, of course, what we call control. These two images, autonomy and control, do a continuous dance. One represents generation, internal regulation, assertion of one's own identity: definition from the inside. The other one represents consumption, input and output, assertion of identity of other: definition from outside.

— FRANCISCO J. VARELA

THE SHORTEST MANUAL for sailboat maintenance says that it all comes down to two rules. If a part of the boat doesn't move, but should, use lubricant. If a part moves, but shouldn't, use adhesive tape.

More generally, whatever needs freedom to function, we should enable its freedom. And whatever doesn't work because it's too loose, we should remove its freedom.

Sailboat maintenance is not that simple, but let's imagine for a moment that it is. We can lubricate the parts that are stuck, but if the boat is not sliding smoothly through the water, do we use lubricant as well? No. It probably doesn't move well because there are sea creatures stuck to the hull. We need to take the boat out of the water, clean it, and apply antifouling to prevent new mussels and oysters attaching to the hull. We free the boat to cut smoothly through the water by taking away the freedom of those little interlopers to settle wherever they want.

There isn't one way of enabling something to move. It's sometimes done by giving, and sometimes by taking freedom. But when and how much? And with machine parts, it's easier. They don't have a mind of their own. Freedom is not the same as autonomy. And what does it mean to fix something if those who have to fix it are part of it? What if it is you who is stuck? And what if you haven't ever moved before?

The Carrot and The Rabbit

Stuck. I'm stuck. I cannot move. I'm fixed to the ground. I always was. All my life. As are all of my kind. I'm a carrot. And carrots cannot move. The rest of the carrots in the garden don't care. They don't want to move. But I do. A lot. That's all I dream of. Not to be always *here*. To be able to go *there* at will. Slowly or quickly, at will. And if I want, to change my mind halfway through, and not go there, but somewhere else. Somewhere far away. I want to go beyond the fence. I want to see the world outside the garden.

Well, I know, that won't happen. Ever! I'm doomed to be stuck. The only motion I get is when my leaves are moved by the wind. Yes, not when I want, but when the wind wants, it moves me. A bit. Back and forth. Feeling more like trembling than moving. That's all I get and all I can hope for. But why do I find motion so attractive? Is it because I have emotion that I can dream of motion? Is emotion a kind of motion? Then maybe, I can use my emotion to turn into something that can move. Let's try.

Trying, trying... Trying some more. Nothing. But if I really focus. If I use all my will, all my emotions.

Now, with all of me, I wish I would turn into something that is able and free to move. Anything that can crawl or walk. Anything. Please! Please! I want it so much!

What's that?! What's going on? Oh, my goodness, something strange is happening to me! My body is changing. Things are moving inside me. That's scary. I'm swelling. I'm getting big and white and ... furry! N-o-o, really?! Why have I turned into a rabbit? Why?

Never mind. I can move now. My dream came true. I can really, actually move. Not only that, I can jump. This is much more than just moving. I don't need to touch the earth all the time. I can briefly stay in the air. Oh, that feels so liberating. I can turn my eyes, my head, my ears, my tail. Amazing. Absolutely incredible! It feels much better than I thought it would. And now I want to run. I want to run as much as I can, as fast as I can, and get as far as I can.

And I'm running. It's me who makes the wind now. I'm running. And I see a new world. Trees, and bushes, and lakes, and other trees, and rocks with strange shapes ... yet not much grass around here.

I'm running. And now there are different trees. The soil is soft and then hard, dry, and then a bit wet. And there are so many smells.

I'm running. But I'm running slower now. And even slower. And breathing heavily. And now I can't run anymore. I'm completely exhausted. And what is that? I feel I need food. I'm hungry. Very, very hungry. I was never hungry before. What did I do when I needed food before, when I was a carrot? Well, nothing. I could not do anything, but I also did not need to do anything. I just stayed there, in the soil, with my leaves in the sun. I didn't need much to live, and all I needed I got right away. Without doing anything. I got sun and air and water and some minerals from the soil. No effort whatsoever. But now that won't work. If I dig a hole in the ground and bury myself up to my neck and pretend my long pointed ears are my leaves, that would only look ridiculous. I'll keep being hungry. No, I'll actually get hungrier. So, I need to find food. I need to go and search and find food. Which I can, because I can move.

But there is nothing to eat around here. And I don't know if there will be any food nearby. The safest choice is to go back. But that's now far away and I'm tired.

To get what I need, I need it for getting to where I can find it.

But I'll get back somehow. Maybe I have some reserve. Yes, there is a bit.

I'm running back slowly now. Luckily, I remember the way back. But it's taking ages. I'm getting hungrier and more tired. Now, after what felt like hours, I'm back in the garden. And there is the food. And the tastiest kind. Carrots! But that's my former pals. Now, what is that? I almost died getting back. The last thing I need now is to deal with moral issues…

From plants to organizations

Unlike plants, animals are detached from their source of food. Animals need to get to it. For that, they must be able to move. But the ability to move comes at a price. It costs energy. And the source of energy is not available right away. They need to find it. While they are freer from the environment, they are at the same time more dependent on it. "To get what I need, I need it for getting to where I can find it."

"Is it because I have emotion that I can dream of motion?" Our carrot was missing the ability to move but magically had emotion and sight. Real carrots don't. The freedom of animals is achieved with a whole package: movement, perception, desire, and higher dependency.

Autonomy is gained at the cost of more dependencies.

Here we see the balance between autonomy and cohesion at the individual level of an animal. But to better deal with the environment, animals get together. They form herds, packs, flocks, and hives. These new forms provide protection, more access to food or ways to buffer it. These benefits are something that an animal cannot achieve on its own. And all of them require coordination. Coordination needs social norms. Norms restrict individual autonomy.

Moving on to the social life of humans, there the game changer is language. It is a remarkable thing! Just by being used, language can develop those that use it and itself within a complex system of feedback loops. Many of these loops are self-referential: we correct language with language, and we talk about language using language. Through language, autonomy found new ways to exert itself and cohesion is achieved in more ways, both in number and sophistication. Language is what boosted the development of new tools, including the ability to print written text and ever easier and cheaper ways to communicate, developing language even further. And it is due to language that more sophisticated forms of social life began to appear. One such form is organizations. But what *are* organizations?

When we see a sweater, we immediately know it's a sweater and not a pile of wool or cotton. We can identify it because it's in front of our eyes and we know what a sweater looks like. We can even touch it. We can see how it is held together, what makes it a sweater and not just many threads.

With organizations, that's not the case. We don't immediately see what holds them together (until we have the right pair of glasses). What is it that, if it is lost, means the organization won't be the same anymore, or not an organization at all? The sweater is designed and made by somebody. The designer and the maker influenced the choice of material, the shape, and the way it was knitted. An organization may have founders, but it is not them who give it its ongoing identity. The organization itself maintains its identity by doing what it does, by having its unique history, structure, and interactions.

It seems that when people do something together, an organization simply emerges. And it is as if it has a mind of its own. The emerged organization lives depending on what people say and do, but it also influences what people say and do, their communications and actions. An organization of sorts might appear even without people deciding to do something together, but just when they are pressed to deal with each other.

You are walking down a narrow corridor and another person is coming towards you. You both stop when you meet, wanting to pass each other. You take a small step to your right and at the same moment the other person takes a step to their left. You are blocking each other. So you step back to your left and inevitably as you do so the other person takes a step to their right. You are in each other's way again. Embarrassed smiles and furrowed brows flit across your faces. This goes on until the synchronicity is broken or until coordination is achieved, depending on how you look at it.

It seems that in such situations, people bring forth something that influences what they do in order to maintain itself, at least for a while. It may not seem right to say that this is an organization, but at least it *has* organization, and one with some form of primitive autonomy. As its cohesion lasts only for a very short time, its autonomy dies quickly as well.

Organization emerges every time a task requires the coordination of more than one person. Here the interest is in formal organizations, those that are established on the basis of decisions and in accordance with some rules or norms.

Formal organizations are different from spontaneous ones in the way they are established, but not so much in the way they maintain their existence. That's why it is useful to see different forms of organization and learn from them. This should be done with caution. We can easily find common patterns which make us want to transfer the positive ones. Analogies might be useful, but using them is prone to the same risks as described earlier about best practices. Since direct transfer is dangerous, we should look for other ways to use that knowledge.

Autonomy in organizations

The balance between autonomy and cohesion is maintained at various levels in a healthy organization. What we have all experienced is the balance at the level between individuals and those they directly interact with. And that's what the next story is about.

Ferenc the Freelancer

It is 7:05 when Ferenc hears his phone alarm for the first time, not counting that it was he who turned over the phone to snooze it at 7:00. A few minutes later he realizes that if he doesn't hurry up, he'll miss the 7:41 train.

He looks at his phone again. Crazy weather is expected today. It's now 5°C and raining but the forecast is for 22°C in the afternoon with an even higher feels-like temperature. Ferenc decides to put on four layers so that he can be comfortable the whole day.

He locks his bicycle at the station at 7:41, but luckily the train is delayed by a couple of minutes.

Ferenc enters the office a few minutes before nine, which will give him enough time to do a few things before the meeting at ten.

Ferenc is a freelancer, yet the way he works with his current contract is not really a client–consultant relationship. He and the regular employees get similar treatment, but he does not enjoy any of their benefits. Apart from that, he's paid for the hours he works. That is so common, yet it puzzles him. At the end of last month when he submitted his timesheet, he thought about what it would be like to submit a worksheet instead, or a value-sheet – if that could have some real meaning beyond the corporate romance of some HR poets.

Armed with a latte and a smile on his face on remembering the pun, "better latte than never", Ferenc starts to review his plan for the day.

He has nine tasks. Six of them are similar to jobs he has done before in a previous assignment with another company. He knows how to do them and can complete them on his own. For them, he doesn't have any dependencies. For the first of the remaining three tasks, he needs to coordinate with other people, and that's what the ten o'clock meeting is about. The last two items are completely new, and he needs to find out how to deal with them. Yet that seems feasible. At least, this is what he's thinking when the email from Emma arrives.

Ferenc's contract is quite clear about the relationships with the employees of his client. They should not imply subordination. Yet, Emma is effectively his boss, regardless of the provisions of the contract or the efforts she takes not to appear so. A pseudo-boss is somehow well suited to a situation with pseudo-consultants. Ferenc, like most of the other freelancers, is treated as more of a substitution for a missing skill set than an actual consultant. One frustrating illustration of this is that in most assignments it's determined not only what he should do but also how he should do it, while it is exactly the missing know-how that was the reason to hire him in the first place.

Emma has been quite absent-minded and apologetic lately.

Now in her email, she apologises for the two requests she is making at such short notice. One is about a report on a software-project evaluation Ferenc did last week. The other is about a meeting from two to three that afternoon. Normally she would send the meeting request right away, but at such short notice, she makes an effort, as a kind of compensation, to first explain in an email how she learned about it just now and why it can't be done another day.

Ferenc is doing quite well with his plan when he goes to that meeting at two, but he might not stay on track if the meeting takes too long. The paradox of short-notice meetings, Ferenc thinks, is that they often generate new tasks, while using up time for tasks that have been planned already. Ferenc had some buffer, but it has already been allocated to the urgent request for the evaluation report, which was originally due next week.

At the end of the meeting, he stays in the room a few more minutes with Emma to let her know how he intends to go about the tasks he considers clear and easy. It is only then that he learns that there is a corporate rule which doesn't allow him to implement the known solution from his previous assignment.

Ferenc decides to go for a short walk and think about how to deal with the situation. Outside it is very hot for the season, just as promised by the weather forecast. He's well prepared for that, but not for the situation at work. When he arrived that morning, he had nine things to do, six of which he had a clear solution for, and enough time to complete all of them. But then there was the report, an extra meeting, and one of the solutions was rejected by a rule he had no clue about. So, from nine items, of which six to do and three to solve and do, he ended up with 12, including the meeting, which took up the time planned for one of the tasks. On his way back to the office, he passes by the café and remembers the latte pun, but this time he doesn't find it funny.

Working for an organization results in a triple loss of freedom. It is about where you want to be, what you want to do, and how you want to do it. The first is being deprived of the choice where you want to be at the moment. Most contracts require you to work in an office, shop, factory, or on a farm. It is not only being physically at a certain place that makes the difference. It is experienced together with the organization's social norms you find yourself complying with, and by doing so, affirming them. We behave differently at work than we do at home. Similar situations bring completely different reactions, and opposite situations can evoke similar emotions.

Imagine a waitress working at a restaurant. One evening she's trying to do her best to serve the whims of a demanding client, and feels disappointed when at the end she gets no tip. She has the next day free and invites friends for dinner. She cooks for them and serves them. One of her friends, very pleased, but also a bit drunk, and probably trying to be funny, tips her with ten dollars. She feels way more offended than the previous evening when she got no tip. But she didn't feel offended when the same friend brought a ten-dollar bottle of wine with him to her house. Yet, she would react differently if she had received a bottle of wine as a tip at the restaurant. All this is *norm*al, but that's only due to the different social *norms* in the two situations, which are otherwise almost identical.

Today there are more jobs that allow working from home. Although some social norms do not need to be observed – on a video conference you can stay in pyjamas from the waist down – you are still adhering to many of the office norms even without being there. And you may work from home and find that a bigger loss of freedom if it's not your choice but because of quarantine.

The second loss of freedom is about what to do. Typically, and no matter where we are in the hierarchy, and even if there is no hierarchy, we don't choose what to do. Maybe what kind of work to do, to a certain extent, but not exactly what. That is assigned or determined externally. In this case, we use "what" to cover both the qualitative and quantitative aspects. While it's often impossible to control *what* is assigned to be done, it could be equally difficult to choose *how much*.

Once the *what* (including *how much*) to do is given, the third loss of freedom is *how* to do it – not as common, yet it frequently occurs. Is it due to the inertia from the industrial age, when the most skilful worker was the direct manager? Or is it the need to control the process and have repeatable results even with a high turnover of employees? Whatever the reason, the *how* seems constantly threatened, especially in big organizations.

There are two things to note here. First is that the distinction between *what* and *how* is a crude one. It's used a lot, but to be useful, it's important to understand its relativity. This relativity is a matter of perspective in both space and time. In an organizational context, we talk in terms of space, not only literally, when our organization has an office in another city, but we also use it metaphorically. We say that somebody is leaving a department, and "leaving" implies metaphorical movement in space. Similarly, it's common to ask that person, "Where are you going?" Both often have actual physical implications, as the other department is probably in a different office or building. But the space dimension is commonly used to describe (metaphorically, though not being always aware of that) the static organizational structure. In our verbal and visual descriptions, organizational units and positions are spread horizontally and vertically.

With this in mind, we can see how *what* is relative in organizational space. *What* for a certain level in focus is the *how* for the level above, and the *why* for the level below. Respectively, the *what* for the level below is the *how* for the level in focus.

In the time dimension, we can see the *why*, the *what*, and the *how* sequentially replacing each other in the network of decisions. If at a certain point we have to choose an option, the reason to make a decision is based on a decision made in the past. We decide on *what* now, based on the *why* decided previously (referred to *what* at the time). Our current *what* decision will drive and enable future decisions. It will be on the *how* from the current perspective, and *what* from its own. Then that future decision will be justified by our *what* as its *why*. If that made you dizzy, take a moment to work it out. It's simpler than it sounds.

That was about the relativity of *what* and *how* in space and in time. The second thing to note is that while the loss of freedom at the level of *what* could be just what is needed for cohesion, the danger comes from the tendency to involve the *how*. When the *how* is tightly coupled with the *what*, organizations lose effectiveness, flexibility, and their natural adaptive capability. This is when autonomy is reduced in order to keep the organization solid, but makes it brittle instead.

But remember that *what* and *how* are relative. Therefore, the *what* that's good for cohesion when not coupled with *how*, is the *how* for the organization it's nested in. Autonomy is needed at every scale. We'll be returning to this point many times.

Capacity, Decisions, and Adaptability

To better understand the pathologies in organizations that don't allow sufficient autonomy, we are going to analyze the problem from three perspectives. These are the perspectives of capacity, decisions, and adaptability. We can call the resulting dysfunctions *capacity pathology*, *decisions pathology*, and *adaptability pathology*. Individually, they cause plenty of harm, but it's their combined effect that threatens organizations' viability. Working together, they damage both current and future performance and reduce the chances for survival in difficult times.

Capacity

The capacity (in the sense of capacity-related) pathology happens at the meeting point between three sets of demands and constraints. One set is that of the environment, another is of the organization, and the third is of the organizational unit in focus – a department, team, or individual. At this meeting point, the organizational and environmental demands and constraints go together on one side of the equation, and those of the individual organizational unit on the other. The capacity pathology is again a matter of disbalance.

In the story of Ferenc, the environmental demands and constraints appear as the tasks he needs to do, but only with their nature, with their qualitative aspect. The quantitative aspect, as well as the actual selection of the tasks, is determined by the organization. Why do environmental demands and constraints appear as Ferenc's tasks? Directly or indirectly, the reason he needs to do what he needs to do comes from outside the organization. It might be a translation of customer demand or a response to a compliance requirement. And then the outcome might directly produce an effect outside. Or it might be used internally and then contribute to a value chain that, at some point, is related to a demand or constraint from a client, partner, or regulatory authority. Of course, it could be a misinterpretation of a demand, something that doesn't need to be done at all, or in the case of a constraint, not actually a restriction. In any case, actual or perceived, there is a component coming from an external source.

In addition to those coming from the environment, there are also constraints, such as the need for coordination, a dependency, which for Ferenc was the reason for the ten o'clock meeting. The meeting appears as a constraint and demand in both its content and duration. It appears as a constraint and demand with its content if during the meeting certain limitations are revealed. Some of the constraints might be on the choices that Ferenc needs to make to do his job. The demand for additional effort might come from these constraints or from other commitments made during the meeting. Various limitations or demands can affect any other participant in the meeting or non-participants who are dependent on the information exchanged and decisions taken. The duration of the meeting is a constraint, for it leaves less time for whatever else needs to be done. Serving internal demands reduces the capacity to meet external demands and deal with external constraints.

Decisions

The second perspective, that of decisions, is a particularly powerful explanatory tool. In fact, most of the problems seen through the lenses of the three balances can be looked at with another pair of glasses. With it, organizations appear as networks of decisions. More about that in the "Productive Paradoxes" chapter. Here, we'll focus only on the decisions-related pathology. This concerns what type of decisions are taken where and by whom.

When organizations are small, they don't have this pathology. There are no big differences in the way people in the team experience everyday challenges. The team is small, and each member is more or less equally exposed to the consequences of their actions. There are also no big position-determined differences on what they see on the horizon when they make decisions about the future.

But when organizations grow, there is a split. Those people who are engaged in everyday operations continue to gather experience in dealing with operational challenges. They can see the consequences of the decisions they make, and they can learn from them. Those responsible for managing now have less knowledge of the operations. At the same time, their decision-making power has increased. While the managers become more powerful, they are more dependent on actions that they don't have direct visibility of.

Often, what happens in operations can only be known through the filter of reports. This creates anxiety, which managers alleviate by using their decision-making power to take more operational decisions, in other words, by reducing operational autonomy. The result is that the company has not just grown in size, it has morphed into a different animal.

Small companies are leopards, agile and fast, with sharp senses. Big companies are giraffes, with a small brain in a head high above, far from where the action is.

Yet this head has an advantage. It can look over the trees. It can see a distant threat or opportunity. Big organizations function better when their leaders limit themselves to the decisions that people in the operations are not well positioned to make, and give those people enough autonomy to make choices using their skills and direct experience. For leaders, knowing is just as important as intelligently managing their own ignorance.

Autonomy is closely related to responsibility, which is another important factor when making decisions. Within the decision pathology, it can work in two opposite directions: to avoid responsibility and to ignore higher-level decisions. When more decisions related to operational matters are taken by people who are *not* directly involved in these matters, those that *are* involved then feel less responsible for their actions. They are simply following orders. The damage doesn't end here. The irresponsible behaviour can spread easily to actions about which the decisions are actually taken by the front-line employees.

The sense of responsibility can also work in the opposite way when some people ignore what is decided higher up so that the job gets done. Sometimes their managers turn a blind eye to this disrespect when they realize that not following orders is what keeps operations effective.

So far, we have seen how the quality of decision-making is prone to deteriorate when the organization grows and the gap between thinkers and doers widens. Something similar happens in time.

Old decisions appear today as rules and plans. Rules are based on decisions made earlier, possibly by people who those affected now don't even know. But if people follow the rules only because rules are there to be followed, that will limit (unnecessarily) their autonomy. The same applies to plans. Plans are packages of decisions on what is to be done, when, and by whom. Those planning decisions were made with the knowledge that was available at that time. When new knowledge is available, the rules or plans should be re-evaluated. Their validity should be challenged. Yet, if plans and rules are constantly challenged, they will not be able to serve their purpose as tools for cohesion.

Before moving to adaptability, one last note related to size. As the distance between thinkers and doers gets bigger when organizations grow, it also gets bigger when organizational units grow. Organizations can remain healthy when they grow if they succeed in balancing autonomy and cohesion at all scales. This means that the size of teams should be kept small.

Adaptability

Organizations remain viable by making small adjustments and larger adaptations to their environment. They need to respond to changing tastes, norms, demands, preferences, legislation, and competition. Organizations constantly change by making a huge number of small adjustments based on the feedback on individual and collective actions. Something is tried, and if it works, it is repeated until it doesn't. Then it is changed as many times as needed until it starts working in the new situation or until the resources are exhausted.

The adjustments are similar to the adaptations in the way they employ perception, action, and memory, but in other ways they are different. Each enacts a different capability. Adjustments enact the capability to sense and respond on matters that give an immediate result. The results are evaluated according to the current dynamics between the organization and its environment. Adaptations enact the capability for novel responses and structural changes.

Imagine an intelligent autopilot for planes. A good flying state is maintained by constantly monitoring certain variables. These variables should be kept within the ranges needed for good flying. For example, if the plane is tilted over to one side, registering this anomaly gives a signal for an action, and its intensity, that needs to be applied until the balance is restored. It's a normal type of response to a normal type of disturbance. This intervention will be successful as long as the action works as expected. But what if the same action that previously brought the plane to the normal flying state produced the opposite effect? Then the second capability can potentially restore the balance. This balance can be restored by either repairing the old regulation mechanism or finding a new way of maintaining the flying state.

With companies, when the level of sales goes down, they respond by changing something. For example, they reduce the selling price. They could cut the price by lowering their costs, the margin, or both. To lower their costs, the company might change suppliers and make the production process more efficient. The changes involved can feel big, yet in terms of adaptation, such changes are small. These small adaptations are what we called "adjustments".

So, sales go down, they lower the price, and sales go up again. But next time sales go down, they lower the price and sales keep going down. Then something different should be done, and if successful, that is a big adaptation. It may involve a fundamentally novel response, for example, changing the business model or creating a new market, which is what Apple did first with the iPod and iTunes, and later with the iPhone.

When we say that something is able to adapt to its environment, the focus is on what "adapt" means (literally it means "to fit"), and less on what that "something" and its "environment" are. We are used to talking about "things", even when we are talking about processes. In our case, this "something" is the organization, but it's not the same "thing" from one moment to the next. It is constantly changing. Some changes are provoked by external stimuli, but others are not. And what is the organization adapting to? Again, not a static environment, but an environment created through the interaction with it, which is also changing through other interactions. So, a changing organization, co-created by the interaction with its environment, is adapting to the environment, co-created through the interaction with it. There is a circular relationship, a self-reference. It's not easy to think about self-reference, but let's try with the following example.

Why is there no software able to predict the behaviour of the stock market? It is because the software cannot consider itself. No matter how intelligent it is, it cannot factor the behaviour of an ecosystem influenced by intelligent agents like itself, which are trying to predict it. This is present in any adaptation. Adapting organizations are adapting to an environment of adapting organizations.

In the story of Ferenc, his adaptive capacity in doing his job for the organization is reduced by organizational constraints. They appear in different forms: as norms, rules, and dependencies on the work and capacity of others. Some constraints come directly from his de facto boss, Emma. She's the one who assigns work to him and controls how the work is carried out. Emma is a provider of constraints in two capacities. First, as representative of the organization, and second, depending on her own constraints and according to her personal understanding of her role. She reduces Ferenc's autonomy in both capacities. She can enact her understanding of her role as much as her own organizational autonomy allows. That enactment is prone to maintain vicious cycles even if her provision of constraints, as representative of the organization, happens to be bringing a minimum healthy amount of cohesion. How do these vicious cycles come about? They did not appear in the story of Ferenc but are quite common and you will recognize them as micromanagement.

You are trying to do your job and your manager is following closely. Why? First, he's feeling responsible for your job, which supports the second reason, his sense of insufficient feedback. Often, there is a third factor: mistrust. These three factors, mixed and spiced with the particular personality of the manager, drive his greater involvement. More involvement can only add partial knowledge due to his capacity limits, both historical and current. The current capacity limits cause the need to filter, summarize, and simplify the information about what's going on, and the historical ones limit the potential to understand. Thus, the increased involvement of your manager in the way you are doing your job doesn't satisfy him. Instead, it further increases the perception of insufficient feedback. Even if there was no initial mistrust, it might appear at this stage. Learning more reveals new areas which are not monitored and triggers even more involvement, now taking the form of micromanagement, only to further increase mistrust.

One of the negative effects of micromanagement is that it leaves less time for useful management and exposes the team to more situations for which it is not prepared. In other words, the micromanagement harms both short-term adjustment and long-term adaptation. In the short term, adaptation is reduced by taking up reaction capacity, as discussed earlier, and in the long term, by missing threats and opportunities while being busy micromanaging.

Micromanaging and mistrust bring new vicious cycles in situations of mass working from home. The need to control is satisfied by increasing the number of meetings, which reduces the time available to do whatever needs to be done or to implement the decisions taken in these meetings. The resulting delays and errors trigger more meetings to address the reasons and decide on the remedies, only to worsen the situation.

To summarize, insufficient autonomy creates capacity problems, negatively affects the quality of operational decisions, and severely harms both short- and long-term adaptability.

But what happens when there is too much autonomy?

Too much autonomy can reduce both effectiveness and efficiency and can drive unethical behaviour at the personal level. Too much autonomy can produce silos at both the personal and organizational level. It can make an organization dysfunctional, and if it reaches extreme proportions, the organization can simply disintegrate.

When there is too much autonomy, an organization works below its potential, and the efforts of each member or team may even block each other. It can be as bad as pulling in opposite directions, like in Krylov's famous fable from 1814:

A Swan, a Pike, and Crab once took their station
In harness, and would drag a loaded cart;
But, when the moment came for them to start,
They sweat, they strain, and yet the cart stands still;
what's lacking?
The load must, as it seemed, have been but light;
The Swan, though, to the clouds takes flight,
The Pike into the water pulls, the Crab keeps backing.
Now which of them was right, which wrong, concerns us not:
The cart is still upon the selfsame spot.

Cohesion

Since most organizational carts do move, it's probably rarely as bad as Krylov describes. Yet if the efforts of all the people working in an organization are represented as vectors, it is easy to see how the sum of them changes depending on how closely they are aligned. Pointing in one direction will maximize the combined effect. Yet, maximizing may not necessarily be a good thing, especially when you read about it in a book about balances. There will be more on that in the following chapters.

The point now is to start creating the habit of associating all cohesion mechanisms with constraints. Whatever brings cohesion, imposes a constraint. With this example, being aligned, pointing in one direction, is a matter of reducing the autonomy of choosing where to point to.

Combining the efforts and pointing in one direction is necessary but not sufficient for cohesion. Take the case of the battering ram, used in ancient times by an attacking force to splinter the wooden gates of a fortification. The log was too big and heavy to be lifted by one person. The combined efforts of several people were needed. Not only that, but they had to swing it in the same direction. These two are necessary but still insufficient conditions for cohesion. And cohesion is needed to achieve the objective of breaking through the gate. Here comes the important part: the warriors using the battering ram must synchronize their movements. One of the soldiers could have coordinated the others by giving them a signal. Or they could have done it together, like when sailors sang songs as they pulled the halyard to raise the heavy mainsail. Even the simplest form of organization requires coordination. The group will only achieve its goal if the warriors batter the gates with the same rhythm, and sailors pull the halyard in sync with each other.

Coordination is a common way to achieve cohesion in organizations. In fact, understood broadly, organizing is a matter of coordination. Many cohesion tools can be seen as tools for coordination: language, uniforms, norms, rules, rituals, meetings, and accounting. A big organization like the Church owes much of its long-term viability to a popular coordination tool: the Church calendar. Doing the same thing at the same time of the year is a coordination mechanism also used by other religions for maintaining their cohesion and viability.

Once an organization is created, formally or informally, it starts a life of its own. Even a very transient organization, like the one emerging when two people try to pass each other in a narrow corridor, has some form of identity. It is alive in the sense that it can influence those individuals whose actions and resulting communication create that identity. It can influence the individuals to maintain the organization regardless of whether that is good or bad for them. Organizations then can be seen as belonging to a certain kind of immaterial species, created and maintained by humans, but not always consciously, not always controlled by them, and not always serving them.

It may come as a surprise, but two other species of this kind are habits and emotions. They are created and maintained by people, they influence whatever is keeping them alive, and they can be beneficial or harmful to those that create them. They are not conscious and do not care. Some bad habits or emotions can kill their creator, and by doing so, kill themselves as well. Which to humans is irrational. While they last, habits and emotions prolong their existence by influencing their creator, as if they care for their own viability. What we call "bad" habits seem to be more successful in stabilizing and persisting than "good" habits, the irony being that the more successful bad habits and emotions are, the sooner they kill their host and themselves.

If we come back to what we commonly call organizations, they are what they are as long as they maintain their identity. This can be achieved in various ways, but all methods and factors have one thing in common: they increase the cohesion and reduce the autonomy. Organizational identity is maintained internally. Yet, by differentiating from their environment, organizations depend on, and use, the environment to maintain that differentiation. They use the environment to get the resources needed for their existence, but can also use it to maintain their cohesion.

Factors and Tools for Cohesion

We can split the ways cohesion is achieved into two categories. The first one is *factors,* and the second one is *tools and capabilities*. Factors bring or demand cohesion but are difficult to influence, while tools and capabilities are what we buy or create and then use to achieve cohesion. To better understand the factors for cohesion, another distinction is useful. If we are aiming at a full picture, we can distinguish three levels of factors – person, organization, market – for the same three levels of cohesion: personal factors for personal cohesion, personal factors for organizational cohesion, and so on until the last combination of market factors for market cohesion. That gives us nine categories. But as we keep our focus on organization, we'll review only organizational cohesion. In this simplified perspective, "personal" refers only to the personal factors for organizational cohesion, and not to the personal factors contributing to personal or market cohesion. Let's use "internal" and "external" for factors that are respectively internal and external for the organization but drive or contribute to organizational cohesion, and not to that of the market.

Internal cohesion factors

Personal factors for cohesion are the forces that drive us to belong to a social group: the need for safety, the need to reduce uncertainty, and the need to increase self-esteem. These cohesion forces are at play for any kind of social group, even those that are not organizations, or those that exist inside or between organizations as some kind of tribe. People have the ability to enact multiple social identities, keeping one of them dominant for a short or long period of time. Even when people belong to a tribe, they are also able to maintain the social identity they get from belonging to the formal organization, and the organization uses that force for its cohesion.

Belonging and social identity influence, and are influenced by, loyalty. Loyalty is a sophisticated emotion and an important cohesion factor. Organizations have invented and evolved tools to increase and maintain loyalty.

Internal *organizational* factors for cohesion are the maintenance of identity, internal dependencies, shared resources, synergies, and efficiency. Once an organization is formed, it starts to maintain its identity on its own. It asserts itself in contrast to its environment. The internal dependencies are direct material or informational flows demanding coordination. They can be of different strengths. Strength here is not related to significance, but only to frequency or proximity of interaction. Strong dependencies are typical of well-structured, routine processes, common in manufacturing and some service areas, such as distribution, banking, insurance, and public administration. Common problems for such processes are the various types of waste, addressed, for example, by Lean methods.

A popular way to handle some types of waste is to replace push processing with pull processing. From the perspective of the Autonomy–Cohesion balance, this is the increase of cohesion by changing autonomy allocation along the flow of work. The shift of control is usually from internal vendors to internal clients. That's for routine processes. But the number of processes that are not routine is increasing nowadays. They are semi-structured or entirely unstructured (aka knowledge-driven processes). These processes are common in healthcare, legal, design, and creative services. With the automation of routine processes, there are now also more knowledge-driven processes in public administration and the finance industry.

Unlike routine processes, the dependencies between knowledge-driven processes are usually revealed only during runtime, and they can be relatively weak. Some processes, structured or not, can run independently in parallel for a long time. But often they may need coordination at a later stage, either when each parallel process produces a component of a product that needs to be assembled, or because the process outputs will have some operational dependencies later on. Well-organized knowledge-driven processes have just enough and the right kind of cohesion to balance the autonomy of the knowledge workers.

The third internal cohesion factor is the shared limited resources. Using the same premises, services, and technology demands coordination from users. For example, we use scheduling software to reserve a meeting room. But the way resources are used by an organized group of people has potential benefits over the usage by a single person. It is a cohesion force for getting together to create an organization as a way of achieving more (being more effective) with less (being more efficient). For example, a single person can't lift a battering ram, serve 50 tables at a restaurant at once, or sail a cargo ship. The cost of a shoe made by a shoemaker can't be as low as that of a shoe from a shoe factory due to economies achieved through specialization, bulk price of materials, and automation.

Tools for cohesion

All these cohesion factors demand cohesion tools, such as goals, standards, rules, methods, decisions, norms, planning, and coordination. There are cohesion tools which are inherited and often improved. And new tools are constantly produced or just emerge spontaneously as a result of repeated interactions.

Cohesion tools help in reducing external complexity at the cost of reducing internal autonomy and increasing internal complexity. Instead of aiming together at many things, or each employee having their own goals, we agree on one or a few. When breaking goals down to smaller goals and means, there is a pressure for rationality, for coherence. What is done at various levels needs to contribute to the end goal. Organizations are expected to be rational. Rationality motivates, rather paradoxically, following rules and standards.

In an organization, everything is either fixed in previously stabilized decisions and habits by means of norms or rules, or it is fixed at every moment by new decisions where there is a choice among several options.

Deciding is always welcome. Selecting one option reduces complexity and enables actions and future decisions. But this enablement also reduces autonomy, since what could be done is reduced to what is decided to be done. Not that there is necessarily rationality, or that the decisions are always followed. Nevertheless, decisions are probably the most important cohesion tool. (We'll see how organizations can be regarded as existing only due to a network of decisions in the "Productive Paradoxes" chapter.)

Planning is another popular tool for cohesion. We agree when to do what, in what sequence, and by whom. It is yet another way to reduce uncertainty, complexity, and organize resources in space and time.

Not having aligned objectives, a structure that supports the strategy, planning, or efficiency, is bad. Yet, being fully aligned or efficient, or following a plan is not necessarily good, as will be discussed in the "Stimuli and Responses" chapter.

All these tools, goals, standards, rules, and plans can be seen as coordination tools. A broader view puts language generally in that category, or specifically, any jargon. A narrower and more conventional usage of "coordination" points to another popular cohesion tool: meetings.

When several people agree to meet, first they reduce the time and space options so that the meeting can happen. They don't meet whenever and wherever but at an agreed time, on an agreed day, and at an agreed place, physical or virtual. Then they use other coordination tools, such as scheduling and room reservation software, the room availability being a matter of shared resource (one of the factors seen previously). At virtual meetings, a video conferencing tool is used, and all participants use the same tool and virtual room. If participants are fully autonomous and each follows their own preference, and one uses Zoom, another Microsoft Teams, and a third Webex, the meeting won't take place.

During the meeting, attendees reduce the available options to what is decided or bring information about rules and standards to be complied with. The fact that meetings are a typical coordination and cohesion tool does not mean they necessarily contribute to any of those. First, meetings are social species as well. They emerge out of communications between people, as do habits, emotions, and other social species. They have a mind of their own; they influence the conditions for their existence as social species. Meetings emerge from the complex dynamic of intentions, preferences, agendas, personalities, emotions, egos, and tribes, acting within the constraints of norms, rituals, and rules. Second, the chance of a meeting being successful depends on the experience of the organizer, the selection of attendees, the preparation, and the moderation. A meeting can be a complete waste of time, it can achieve its purpose, or it can bring unexpected results out of serendipity or by being an exchange outside the functional silos. And last, the success of a meeting depends on the Autonomy–Cohesion balance before, during, and after the meeting.

The cohesion tools in the story of Ferenc were the two meetings (the planned and unplanned one), the corporate rule preventing him from applying one of the envisaged solutions, and the required software evaluation report.

So far, we have seen personal and internal cohesion factors. For the latter, we also discussed some of the most common cohesion tools. Now we'll look at cohesion factors that come from outside.

External cohesion factors

What is it that brings cohesion in an organization, without being part of it? Three prominent examples of external cohesion factors are the market, a single technology supplier, and a common enemy.

There might be no internal dependencies between two departments, no input/output relationships, no shared resources, and no collaboration of any kind. Yet those that pay and those that use their services can be one and the same or connected in some way. It could be because of geographical proximity, using the same social media, or through any chain of intermediaries. And that external connectivity can – and often does – make the two departments influence each other positively or negatively. It is an example where cohesion is realized externally through the chain: department A has client A, who talks to client B of department B. The market provides a medium for communication. As such, although external, it is, in fact, a direct cohesion factor.

The market can also play the role of indirect cohesion factor by providing models for relations. Organizations often try to copy or interpret market models for internal use, based on the belief that they will improve the organizational performance and the quality of their products and services. Such examples are internal service agreements, often involving actual payments and competition between internal and external providers. A related example is the trend for some public sector organizations to be run like private companies.

Organizations nowadays are very much dependent on

technologies. They often struggle to make different software applications work better with each other. Such integration efforts involve huge investments. And take time. In the case of software, by the time an application integration is achieved, it already needs to be updated. The need for updates is caused by a change of software versions, legislation, or business requirements. It then seems attractive to purchase different dependent components from the same vendor. This brings a lot of benefits: a simpler procurement process, a lower total cost of ownership, lower training costs, minimal or no integration efforts, and easier planning. But at the same time, it creates a dependency on the strategy and fate of that vendor. The vendor might not use some new technologies that the client organization can benefit from. Or it might add capabilities important for some other clients, but not for the client organization in question. The capabilities that the organization needs are often offered by competing suppliers, but the cost of changing the vendor is too high. Such vendor lock-in also exposes the client organization to the risks associated with mergers, acquisitions, and bankruptcy of the vendor. Another negative effect is the overall discouragement of competition and the reduced chances of survival of small and potentially innovative vendors.

A common enemy can act as a unifier who can catalyse self-organization and adaptability in which the coordination is done without too much sacrifice of individual autonomy. When the unifier is gone, the need for coordination is no longer urgent. It decreases if the missing external cohesion factor is not compensated for. That is perceived as a loss of individual autonomy and brings a stream of compensatory communications, which, slowly or quickly, erodes the cohesion. This is observed, for example, in political parties and NGOs.

Some external and internal factors can play a double role in the Autonomy–Cohesion balance. Let's take *trust*, for example. As seen earlier, one of the factors for the increased involvement of managers is mistrust. This makes trust a factor for autonomy. And indeed, it empowers and enables the people who are trusted to use their autonomy. However, trust can also be a cohesion tool. This is certainly the case in virtual teams.

The Autonomy–Cohesion balance looks different for different types of operations. That's why benchmarks and recipes don't work. If there is a way to measure the balance, then it would look quite different for an infantry soldier, compared with a paratrooper, and compared with a spy. In such a comparison, a spy can appear too autonomous, while in fact, not having sufficient autonomy, and a soldier can appear too restricted, but it could be that he or she has too much autonomy for the particular structure and situation.

Nested Autonomy–Cohesion balances

The Autonomy–Cohesion balance needs to be maintained at different levels. "Levels" is a spatial metaphor applied for an organization often referring to positions and units in their formally established functional boundaries. These formally established boundaries are like lines drawn in the sand. The actual walls are built by what the members placed inside the contours do. They are built from inside by what people say and do to maintain we/them distinctions. And they are reinforced from outside by separate budget allocation, packaged together with assigned responsibility and allowed autonomy.

Levels imply vertical hierarchy. However, internal organizational boundaries appear in both hierarchical and flat(ter) organizations. It is more useful to imagine organizations as made up by smaller nested organizations, similar in some ways, different in others. Thus, moving from one level to another should not be imagined as going up or down. It should be imagined as zooming in or out, such as when viewing a fractal such as the Mandelbrot set (if you haven't seen an animation of zooming into the Mandelbrot set, there are plenty available on YouTube). Here "levels" will be used in that broader sense.

Let's now zoom so that our vantage point is that of a team leader. From this perspective, our focus in the organization is the team, and the higher level refers to the bigger common organization, a department, for example.

A team leader is concerned with the cohesion of her team. Another concern might be to create an environment where each team member has sufficient autonomy (and it should be if she is a good team leader). Her inward efforts will be primarily towards cohesion. The team should act like one. However, her outward concern will be for higher autonomy. A more autonomous team is bound by fewer constraints and will have more options to choose from when carrying out its work. It will be better positioned when it comes to capacity, decisions, and adaptability, as shown earlier. Then, of course, the coordination of this team with other teams is of concern for the higher organizational level and even at the one in focus, if there are direct dependencies. At each level, the primary inward-looking concern is that of cohesion, and the outward-looking one is that of autonomy. If the balance between autonomy and cohesion is maintained at one level but not at another, especially if that's the next one up or down, the performance and adaptability of both the level in focus and the next one up or down will suffer.

I have observed a lot of cases of organizational units maintaining good Autonomy–Cohesion balance that are still dysfunctional because that balance was not maintained at the higher level. For example, in many public sector and educational organizations, the freedom of some managers to hire and fire is very limited. Even when their department is capable of maintaining a good Autonomy–Cohesion balance, that doesn't enable good performance if this balance is not maintained at the next level up.

Paradoxically, that becomes a stabilizing factor. Organizational evolution ensures that these positions are taken up by people who don't make good decisions to hire and fire anyway, in case they were allowed to do so independently.

Another, and recently widespread example, are the so-called Agile practices. Some Agile practices are counterproductive, due to misapplication, cult, commercial interests, and not being agile about being Agile. Others work. And when they do, they are excellent examples of maintaining the Autonomy–Cohesion balance at the team level. The standard cohesion tools, such as requirements, plans, meetings, and reports, are replaced with stories, sprints, Kanban boards, stand-ups, and retrospectives. These tools bring a type of cohesion which does not reduce autonomy to a level affecting adaptability.

Yet, while these practices produce good results, the results are local. The Autonomy–Cohesion balance is not maintained at the next level. The local successes are not problematic for just being local. They create local optima, proliferate silos, and make corporate cohesion even more challenging. The corporate concerns for cohesion and interoperability have no way to appear in each Agile team, or if they appear, they do so as compliance requirements. That's not something one can be passionate about, see as a relevant story, or be willing to sacrifice the next prototype for. The emergence of practices, such as Scaled Agile Framework (SAFe) and Large-Scale Scrum (LeSS) are trying to address this problem. So far they have a lot of reported success, but not much real success.

The symptoms of organizational diseases are often misattributed, but it is done convincingly enough to support serious structural and strategic decisions. For example, the effects of not maintaining the Autonomy–Cohesion balance might make one organization take centralization actions and another decentralization actions. And often, one and the same organization, if it lives long enough, will swing between centralization and decentralization. Or, it may think of something as a new form of decentralization, which in fact, contributes to ultra-centralization, but is not seen as such from the viewpoint of decision-makers. Summing up my observations of several big organizations (private and public), the story goes like this:

Stage 1. Realizing the variety of challenges and the dependency on the context, the organization started to decentralize, giving more autonomy to the subsidiaries.

Stage 2. Years later they found big inefficiencies. We'll look at one area, that of information systems, where it's easier to see the patterns. A lot of expensive applications turned out to have duplicated capabilities. Application silos have formed, requiring never-ending integration investments.

Stage 3. The solution was centralization: one data centre for the whole organization, selecting the best out of similar applications and make it a corporate service, establishing tighter IT governance. This actually resulted in higher cost, slower processes, reduced adaptive capacity, and lower service quality.

Stage 4. The restrictions, the slower processes, and the reduced flexibilities pushed the organizational pendulum to decentralization and back when the old problems reappeared.

Stage 5. The new solution to this was the move to the cloud. This was seen as decentralization for two reasons. First, because the data of the subsidiaries was not in the corporate data centre anymore. And second, although the central IT governance retained a lot of control, the subsidiaries could negotiate some of their specific requirements directly with the cloud service providers.

However, this was, in fact, ultra-centralization.

To understand why this was (and is) ultra-centralization, we need to zoom out and see the bigger picture. Let's say there are 2,000 big organizations in the world, and on average, each has ten divisions. So, following stages 1–5 as above, the overall centralization is from 20,000 organizations hosting their own data to 2,000 to 2. The last two are the most common cloud services, Azure (Microsoft) and Amazon Web Services (AWS). That tremendously increases the vulnerability of whole economies, not even counting the overall damage coming from the tight data–application coupling.

Just as ultra-centralization can be disguised as centralization, an actual centralization could bring more autonomy, which we would normally expect from decentralization. Local authorities in the United Kingdom used to be responsible for the local education authority which ran and, when necessary, built new schools. With the free school policy, anyone can apply to the Department for Education (DfE) to open a school and that school is much more autonomous than the existing maintained schools (those still run by the local authorities), but it is funded directly by the DfE. This shows again that centralization/decentralization is the wrong dilemma.

When "centralized" is used to describe an organization, it often becomes associated with being "too hierarchical". Such a qualification implies that the balance seems shifted towards cohesion, and that such organizations are slow to adapt to environmental changes. It is often the case, but we should be careful. "Too hierarchical" might mean two different things. One could refer to a command-and-control kind of establishment with autocratic management, and the other could refer to having too many reporting levels. For example, in some big organizations, over 20% of the employees are managers. That could be due to having too many organizational levels, and as such, an example of "too hierarchical" used in the second sense. Or it might be because they operate in many territories, or because although there is only one level and the units at that level are small and many. In any case, "too hierarchical" might be triggered by an Autonomy–Cohesion disbalance but won't point towards which extreme and where.

For a handy example of a good Autonomy–Cohesion balance, you need look no further than the World Wide Web. The first connection on the internet was in 1969, but it wasn't anything interesting or influential. It was just a network between a few computers located at a distance from each other. Users needed specialized technical knowledge to connect to a remote computer and find and retrieve files. The advent of hypertext systems improved that. Yet, hypertext systems were used locally. What brought the big change was integrating one of them with other technologies and making them all available as open standards. The World Wide Web was born of the marriage between HTML and the internet, and that union completely changed the lives of billions of people in the following decades. It gave unprecedented autonomy and affordability to share and to get information.

On the web, everyone was free to say whatever they wanted (autonomy) as long as it was shared using the agreed standards (cohesion). These standards ensured a uniform way to publish, identify, and access documents on the web. And it enabled individuals and companies to invent various web applications (autonomy), which could be widely used only when they conformed to the agreed standards (cohesion). A lot of websites appeared, offering more information and functionality, enabled by better devices and browsers, which increased the possible uses of the internet, which in turn increased the proliferation of new business models and applications. An ecosystem with a well-designed and maintained Autonomy–Cohesion balance is conducive to such virtuous cycles.

Summary

Cohesion means an "act or state of sticking together". It is about forming a unity. Without cohesion, instead of a stone, there will be dust; instead of a house, there will be a pile of bricks; and instead of an organization, there will just be individuals minding their own business.

When something loses cohesion, it's no longer what it was. It's broken, it's not working.

When the molecules of a stone are not sufficiently attracted, it's no longer a stone. To build a house, we don't only need bricks and beams, we also need mortar and nails, knowledge and skills. For different structures, we need to know how the forces of tension, compression, and torsion work. Only then can we ensure the cohesion of a house.

But once a house is built, it stays put. That's not the case with organizations. They are dynamic, they constantly change, and they behave as if they have a mind of their own. Their cohesion is multidimensional and complex. And maintaining it is not an easy task. What's even more difficult is to have just enough of the healthy kind of cohesion.

Cohesion in organizations is due to various factors. Some are personal and ancient, such as the drive for belonging and safety, or the need to reduce uncertainty and increase self-esteem. Apart from the personal, there are organizational factors for cohesion because we have shared resources, and we depend on each other to do the work. Failing to deal with the organizational factors leads to misalignment, bottlenecks, and other kinds of waste. There are also external factors for cohesion, such as the medium of the markets.

The personal cohesion factors contribute to cohesion, and yet they need to be reinforced with methods for increasing loyalty and trust. In contrast, organizational factors do not contribute, but demand cohesion. And we respond to this demand with various coordination tools, such as goals, standards, rules, methods, decisions, norms, scheduling, and planning.

Whatever gives cohesion, adds constraints. When there are too many internally imposed constraints that reduce autonomy, organizations become rigid and slow to adapt.

When there is too much cohesion, there is not enough autonomy for individuals, teams, and departments. Insufficient autonomy reduces the available capacity, the quality of decisions, and the organization's adaptability both in the short and long term.

Too much autonomy, however, produces silos, inefficiencies, and can make organizations dysfunctional.

So we need to balance autonomy and cohesion. At different scales and in different situations, the balance may look and work differently. We need the sensibility to detect the patterns. This we can do by developing the habit of seeing situations and organizations through Autonomy–Cohesion glasses.

Having more autonomy will bring more diversity in an organization, more ways to handle the stimuli of the environment. At the same time, it is the cohesion which makes an organization more solid and often more stable. It seems that the Autonomy–Cohesion balance is closely related to the next balance, Diversity–Stability.

NOTES

1. Freedom is not the same as autonomy.

Freedom is something given, and autonomy is internally maintained. The US Constitution is an example:

> *[T]he United States Constitution grants and ensures particular rights and freedoms. The First Amendment grants the freedom of religion, speech, the press, and assembly. The Second Amendment grants the freedom to keep and bear arms. The Fifth Amendment grants the freedom to remain silent. And so forth. These freedoms are intended to buttress against the power of the State. But, ironically, these freedoms actually institute and enforce the power of the State. In other words, we are free to enact these freedoms as long as the dominating power—in this case, the State—grants us these rights.* (Del Gandio, 2012)

2. The freedom of animals is achieved with a whole package: movement, perception, desire, and higher dependency.

Animals are not directly linked to their source of food. There is a distance they need to span. For that, they are equipped with three abilities: to perceive the distance, to want to span it, and to be able to. In the words of Hans Jonas:

> *[P]erception presents object "not here but over there"; desire presents the goal "not yet but to come": motility guided by perception and driven by desire turns* there *into* here *and* not yet *into* now. (Jonas, 2001)

The freedom endowed to animals is paradoxical. It is, in fact, a "needful freedom":

> *The privilege of freedom carries the burden of need and means precarious being* (ibid.).

3. When we see a sweater, we immediately know it's a sweater and not a pile of wool or cotton.

Well, it might be that some designs, at a distance, would challenge "immediately".

4. With organizations, that's not the case. We don't immediately see what holds them together.

As Nils Brunsson put it, "although organizations are manifold, rich, and powerful, no one has ever seen an organization" (Brunsson, 2009). Organizations are what they are, not due to their substance but due to their form.

5. As its cohesion lasts only for a very short time, its autonomy dies quickly as well.

Such an encounter, as described by Cuffari et al., has "an *interactive normativity*, different from the individual norms" (Cuffari, Ezequiel, & Hanne, 2014), emphasis in the original. The cohesion is achieved through the new norms. These norms are different from the norms of the two individuals. The interaction achieves its own autonomy. It lasts as long as it's able to modulate the behaviour of the two individuals.

Such an interaction is typically explained as oscillation caused by a synchronized overreaction, but that view is ignoring the emergent autonomy. However, it has its merits from a regulation perspective, and such a perspective is used in the chapters "Stability and Diversity" and "Stimuli and Responses".

6. Similar situations bring completely different reactions, and opposite situations can evoke similar emotions.

When working in organizations, the loss of freedom is from both what is left out and what is accepted:

> *The firm is a social system, which consists of people who forgo certain interests (to spend their day as they would prefer, for instance) in the interests of the organization and who accept rules of behaviour that would surprise anyone observing such behaviour outside the organisation.* (Baecker, 2006)

7. Is it due to the inertia from the industrial age, when the most skilful worker was the direct manager?

Patrick Hoverstadt points out in *The Fractal Organization,* that if at the beginning of the twentieth century it was estimated that 95% of workers could not do their job as well as their immediate boss, this has now reversed.

> *Nowadays, it is normally the case that staff understand how to do their job better than their bosses and management is seen as a separate skill in its own right, not just something that the best operators will acquire through osmosis.* (Hoverstadt, 2008)

8. With it, organizations appear as networks of decisions.

Following Luhmann's social systems theory, organizations are made of, and constantly reproduced by, a network of decisions (Seidl, Becker, & Luhmann, 2005). Decisions are paradoxical in nature. How so will be explained in the last chapter, "Productive Paradoxes". The deparadoxization of decision is the driving force of the organizations and it happens both in space, by the functional differentiation, and in time, by postponing one of the conflicting elements.

9. [E]ach member is more or less equally exposed to the consequences of their actions.

This changes when organizations grow. It's not only the decision-makers who move away from the action. This happens with most people involved in fat support functions.

> *Bureaucracy is a construction by which a person is conveniently separated from the consequences of his or her actions.* (Taleb, 2018)

The public sector organizations have that "construction" earlier, and when they grow, the gap is usually bigger than in similar-size companies from the private sector.

10. But when organizations grow, there is a split.

Coordination is easy in small companies.

> *For example, a small, five-person company has no trouble coordinating its activities. But as it grows to 20, 30, 40 people, it becomes more difficult to coordinate the work. So the company initiates a Monday morning "all-hands" meeting, where everybody shares what they are working on and their plan for the coming week. As more people join the company, the Monday meeting becomes overly lengthy, and people become frustrated because they spend so much time talking about work that they don't have enough time to complete their projects.* (Gray, 2014)

And then there is a split into thinkers and doers, and as the company grows, the gap between them widens. In the words of Luc Hoebeke, "tinkers (thinking in action), appear to be more effective in joint action than thinkers (thinking to delegate actions)" (Hoebeke, 2014).

11. For leaders, knowing is just as important as intelligently managing their ignorance.

Knowing more does not reduce what is not known. As there will always be things which will not be known, instead of attempting to reduce ignorance with more information, it is more efficient to intelligently manage ignorance by self-limiting involvement (Knudsen, 2017).

12. [T]he gap between thinkers and doers widens.

This is just a shorthand. It doesn't mean that doers stop thinking and thinkers stop doing.

13. This means that the size of teams should be kept small.

Luc Hoebeke introduced and defined the concept of span of relations:

> *The span of relations is the maximum number of people able to attribute a shared meaning to the system of relations they develop through the system of activities in which they are involved.* (Hoebeke, 1994)

14. Adjustments enact the capability to sense and respond on matters which give an immediate result.

Sometimes sensing is not sufficient for sense-making and adaptation. In complex situations, there are no obvious causal relations. What can be perceived as a result of the interactions of many agents? There is no apparent causality. Kurtz and Snowden call this phenomenon *retrospective coherence* (Kurtz & Snowden, 2003). Emergent patterns cannot be predicted. Causality is coherent in retrospect and not repeated.

> *Once a pattern has stabilized, its path appears logical, but it is only one of many that could have stabilized, each of which also would have appeared logical in retrospect.* (ibid.)

The decision model in this situation should be to provoke the patterns to become more visible, and once they are, respond by trying to stabilize the desirable ones and destabilize the undesirable ones.

15. It may involve a fundamentally novel response, for example, changing the business model or creating a new market, which is what Apple did first with the iPod and iTunes, and later with the iPhone.

It wasn't the actual iPod device which created the market, but the new business model, which was introduced with the iTunes Music Store in 2003. It wasn't only a virtual replacement of physical music stores, available in your pocket 24/7. It offered one solution for purchasing and consuming music. That uniqueness guaranteed a monopoly for some time until other similar vendors, such as Spotify entered the market.

For the iPhone, it was more of a creating a new market for new types of devices, but it changed a larger ecosystem and created the symbiotic market of mobile apps.

16. [No organization is] the same "thing" from one moment to the next. It is constantly changing.

In the interaction between an organization and its environment, there are patterns that look just like another instance of the same activity: processing an order, hiring an employee. But this is the same kind of illusion as when somebody steps in a river and then stepping again looks like doing the same thing. As Heraclitus is believed to have said, "no man ever steps in the same river twice, for it's not the same river and he's not the same man."

17. The current capacity limits cause the need to filter.

When the rich in Rome had to deal with the problems of people and reached their capacity limits, they put gates with grids and appointed guardians, the proto-clerks, at the gates to decide who to let in. This is the birth of bureaucracy. The word *cancelli,* meaning "gates" (retained in contemporary Italian) and "crossed bars", appears today as the root for "office" in some Slavic languages (Slovak: *kancelária*, Bulgarian: *канцелария*, Serbian: *канцеларија*), and is the origin of *chancellor* and *cancel* in English (Harper, 2018).

18. Too much autonomy [...] can drive unethical behaviour at the personal level.

A recent article (Lu, Joel, Vardi, & Weitz, 2017) reported that high job autonomy increased unethical behaviour observed across five studies. As "job autonomy also predicted job satisfaction and creativity", the overall conclusion of the authors is that job autonomy is a double-edged sword.

19. [L]ike in Krylov's famous fable from 1814.

Some of the fables of Ivan Andreyevich Krylov are based on those of La Fontaine, but "The Swan, a Pike, and the Crab" is original (Harrison I. H., 1883). In later translations it appeared more often as "Swan, Pike and Crawfish":

> *Once Crawfish, Swan and Pike*
> *Set out to pull a loaded cart,*
> *And all together settled in the traces;*
> *They pulled with all their might, but still the cart refused to budge!*
> *The load it seemed was not too much for them:*
> *Yet Crawfish scrambled backwards,*
> *Swan strained up skywards, Pike pulled toward the sea.*
> *Who's guilty here and who is right is*
> *not for us to say-*
> *But anyway the cart's still there today.*

20. The point now is to start creating the habit of associating all cohesion mechanisms with constraints.

Here I use "mechanism" in the sense of "natural or established process by which something takes place or is brought about", corresponding to the second definition from the Oxford English Dictionary. Yet the risk of associating "mechanism" with "mechanistic" remains. It is additionally increased by the many Cybernetics references. While Cybernetics finds similarities between human systems (both biological and social) and machines to the point of studying humans as machines, they are different kinds of systems and analogies can be misleading.

21. [T]wo other species of this kind are habits and emotions.

One of the trends in philosophy and psychology to see habits as self-organizing structures (Barandiaran & Di Paolo, 2014), is being followed and further developed by the enactive school in cognitive science. Some recent work, using sensorimotor-habit-based controllers, demonstrates that habits "care" about their viability (Egbert & Cañamero, 2014). Finding autonomy maintained in domains different that of the biochemical organism, help explain why we care about norms not related to our viability, such as the way we lift a glass of water, or why we engage in unhealthy behaviour, such as smoking (Di Paolo, Cuffari, & De Jaegher, 2018). And it's not only habits. Studies on emotions confirm that they are similar kind of "species":

> *[E]motional episodes correspond to specific self-organizing forms [...] that recruit or entrain various processes (neural, muscular, autonomic, etc.) into highly integrated configurations or patterns.* (Colombetti, 2014)

22. Once an organization is formed, it starts to maintain its identity on its own. It asserts itself in contrast to its environment.

At the same time, this also balances out at market level. Organizations assert their identity and make it clear what it means to belong to it and to be outside. They try to be different and unique. But in doing so, they want to make rational decisions and improve. This way, various management standards and best practices are born. However, following standards and best practices makes organizations remarkably similar (Dimaggio & Powel, 1983).

23. Common problems for such processes are the various types of waste, addressed, for example, by Lean methods.

Lean identifies seven types of waste: inventory, overproduction, extra processing, transportation, waiting, motion, and defects. Initially applied only in manufacturing, this practice quickly spread out to the service industries. In software development, for example, Lean principles influenced Agile development. Agile teams address inventory waste (which is minimizing work in progress), by trying to find the right granularity of work items, minimize dependencies, and keep short-cycle planning. The overproduction, manifested in developing unnecessary features, is reduced by frequent interaction with the client through the whole project and by delivering working prototypes at the end of each iteration. Non-value-added activities and hand-offs, the wastes of extra processing and transportation, respectively, are addressed with cross-functional, co-located teams and by creating conditions for self-organizing where the most effective and efficient way of working emerges. Waiting (waste 5) and frequent switching of tasks (waste 6) are reduced by limiting the work in progress, delivering early and frequently, and ensuring a clear understanding of each work item and what it takes to complete it within the increment in which it is planned. Defects (waste 7) are reduced by ensuring quality in the development process as opposed to investing in detection and correction activities.

24. [New cohesion] tools are constantly produced or just emerge spontaneously as a result of repeated interactions.

Frequent interaction between people brings agreement on naming things, doing things, and on what is fair. These conventions improve coordination and stimulate the generation of more conventions. Institutions, authorities, and incentives can influence the appearance and stabilization of conventions, but they can also emerge spontaneously (Centola & Baronchelli, 2015).

25. Rationality motivates, rather paradoxically, following rules and standards.

Rationality is accepted as the only right way to make decisions and manage organizations. Yet, it is would only be possible if we could predict the future (including the stability of our preferences). For only then we can see which actions logically result in achieving our goals. This leads to discrepancies between what we want, say, and do (Brunsson, 2006). And then, to be better at rationality, we follow rules and standards which are often external (such as quality standards, management methodologies and practices). But even when they are internal, they don't take into account the concrete logic of expecting that certain decisions and actions, in the current context, will lead to the desired outcome. This way, while aiming for rationality, based on internal logic, we do just the opposite by following standards which have a logic of their own (ibid.).

26. A related example is the trend for some public sector organizations to be run like private companies.

Public organizations and markets try to resemble each other, the former adopting market models, the latter increasing regulation.

27. It then seems attractive to purchase different dependent components from the same vendor.

It is not just attractive, it is actively encouraged, unfortunately. The fourth of the highly influential management principles of Deming – Deming's 14 Points – says that the aim to minimize the total cost of ownership should be achieved by moving towards a single supplier (Deming, 2000).

28. This is certainly the case in virtual teams.

There are more teams that are not co-located nowadays. Often, the team members of virtual teams have no previous history of working together. And the trust – while it is needed more than in the co-located and temporary virtual teams – is more difficult to achieve. In fact, as trust depends on familiarity, it should be impossible. Yet, a phenomenon which some authors call "swift trust" is observed (Meyerson, Weick, & Kramer, 1995). It can be an important factor for team cohesion (Crisp & Jarvenpaa, 2013).

29. They create local optima, proliferate silos, and make corporate cohesion even more challenging.

Although the Agile practices have spread outside software development, it is still their main territory. One of the negative effects is that Agile practices reinforce the application-centric mindset, which has caused a lot of damage to organizations and still does. Agile teams have, for example, little motivation to apply common standards and data models (McComb, 2018).

30. Let's say there are 2,000 big organizations in the world.

DBpedia agrees with such a guess.

This query (http://bit.ly/org20Kempl) will give you the organizations that have over 20,000 employees and are currently in the DBpedia dataset. DBpedia gets the data from Wikipedia, and it is safe to assume that most big companies have a Wikipedia page about them. The actual number is more likely to be bigger, which even better illustrates the point about this being a case of ultra-centralization.

31. [T]he last two are Azure (Microsoft) and Amazon Web Services (AWS).

This might have changed significantly by the time you read this, but at the time of writing these two vendors had over 62% of the cloud market (Gartner, 2019).

32. [N]ot even counting the overall damage coming from the tight data–application coupling.

The application-centric mindset has created a huge amount of waste in big organizations and continues to do so (McComb, 2018). It creates even bigger damage in the whole ecosystem by turning the web into a centralized system, conducted by a few big participants as Facebook and Google, with severe consequences for privacy, pluralism, and the spread of misinformation. This phenomenon has been analyzed from different perspectives, e.g. see Zuboff (2019) for analysis from an economic perspective and Verborgh (2017) from a technical perspective.

2

STABILITY AND DIVERSITY

Organization resides between smoke and crystal just as it resides between conversation and text. Organization is talked into existence when portions of smoke-like conversation are preserved in crystal-like texts that are then articulated by agents speaking on behalf of an emerging collectivity. Repetitive cycles of texts, conversations, and agents define and modify one another and jointly organize everyday life.

— Taylor and Van Every, *The Emergent Organization*

The second pair of glasses is for observing stability and diversity. Stability and diversity are important for organizations. That's easy to see. What is difficult to understand is how they form a balance. In a way, there are three different balances involved. Different, yet somehow the same. And the key to understanding it is exactly in these two words: *different* and *same*.

Three-in-one

The concepts of stability and diversity operate in different dimensions. Stability is sameness in time, while diversity is difference in space.

When we say that the oil price is stable, we mean that it doesn't change much over a certain period. Same for the temperature, sea level, or people's behaviour. It's all about change in time. Try searching for "is stable" in the news, and you'll mostly get three types of results: about currency or growth rate; referring to the political situation somewhere; or concerning the condition of a person in a hospital after an accident.

In contrast, diversity is used for difference in space. It is for having different things within something uniting or containing them. We use it for restaurant offerings, for teams when their members are of different ethnicity, age, and gender. We also hear the word "biodiversity" frequently used in ecological contexts.

The balance between stability and diversity can be observed in the dimensions that they typically operate in language. It can also be observed the other way around, with stability in space and diversity in time. But it becomes really interesting when, in highly adaptive organizations, more diversity of the right kind can restore stability when it is disturbed. This will become clearer when *same* and *different* are applied in time and space. Now let's start with the simplest case, taking only *sameness* and only *time*.

When *sameness* is used only in time, then stability can be seen as a balance in itself. It can be applied to any other balance being maintained over time. The opposite of stability is instability. Instability refers to stability; it is about stability. A plane flight is unstable when there is turbulence. Unstable is used to describe a flight when its stability is disturbed by turbulence. We use instability only when it is possible to restore normal operation. We don't apply it when there is a plane crash.

This is the first hidden balance: Stability (in time) – Instability (in time). Or, to use the other two words, maintaining *sameness*, when it is challenged by *difference*. Maybe a more appropriate way of writing this variation is with stability in the middle:

instability – stability – instability

Note that, while trying to see stability as a balance in itself, diversity appeared anyway, disguised as instability.

It seems that using *same* and *different* in *time* works so far. Perhaps it is because we allowed another pair to sneak in: *good* and *bad*. Stable is good, unstable is bad. Now, since good and bad have been revealed, let's play with them. Let's try, for example, to see stability as bad (why not?). Then the balance will be: Stability (in time, is bad) – Diversity (in time, is good). While people who are already comfortable wearing Stability–Diversity glasses can easily see it that way, it won't be the case for people who are not. For them, something like "Rut–Innovation" works better. And indeed, when organizations do the same things the same way while expecting better results, they won't get them. Worse, when organizations do things the same way while their environment changes, they are increasingly unable to achieve even the same results.

A more neutral way to talk about this flavour of the balance is Stability–Change. The biased versions, Stability–Instability and Rut–Innovation, retain their utility in some contexts.

Just as it was with Autonomy–Cohesion, the scale matters here as well. Good and bad in "Stability (in time, is bad) – Diversity (in time, is good)" should be understood only at a certain scale. The way it is stated above implies the need for innovation. After the innovation is implemented, the new state has to be stabilized, at least for a while.

Now, here is where the scale makes the difference. During that period, the change brought by the innovation should settle in. The changed organization should find new stability. The balance for that settling period should then be seen as "Stability (in time, is good) – Diversity (in time, is bad)".

We tried "Stability is bad". If we do the same with difference in time, this will form "Innovation is bad". It may sound strange, but it is an actual strategy for some healthcare practices, as well as for companies like General Motors, Ford, and American Airlines. It even has a name, *exnovation*. Exnovation does not completely object to innovation, but promotes a balanced approach to it.

So far, we've seen Stability–Diversity in time, which can be looked at as Stability–Change, Stability–Instability, or Rut–Innovation. The first perspective is neutral, the second is when we need to maintain stability, and the third is when stability is maintained in spite of the need for change. Now, the analogue for Diversity in *space* is to look at it as a balance itself. This will reveal the second hidden balance, Diversity–Homogeneity. Too much diversity might be bad for stability in some cases, in others, the more the better. There will be more on that later.

And there is a third hidden balance between stability and diversity, where stability operates in *time* and diversity in both *space* and *time*. This balance sounds more complex, but there is an easy way to understand it. We will see this later when looking at one of the evolutionarily most advanced organizations and how it works. For now, we will make do with an abstract description: having more diversity (in space) or trying out different things (diversity in time) could be very important for maintaining stability (in time). However, too much diversity alone, or in the wrong context, can destabilize.

If the Stability–Diversity balance seemed strange when you first thought of it, seeing it as three-in-one balances has probably changed the way you think about it. It may still be unclear without examples. They will come later. Then, if you don't need this three-in-one device anymore, you can throw it away. But to prepare for that, we now need to look closer at Stability and Diversity, first separately and then together.

Stability...

It is a good practice when introducing a concept to start with a definition. Definitions bring stability. But I'm not going to do that. You may have your own understanding of it. That means more diversity, which is fine. But we also need stability. However, instead of forcing it with a definition, we'll let the concept self-stabilize. How are we going to do that? We'll start with a few simple observations. Then we'll get into more sophisticated cases. The notion of stability that will emerge may confirm, enrich, or contradict your previous understanding. Then the notion may change when other observations are added. But at some point, we will reach an understanding that's both rich and stable.

The concept of stability is widely applicable. Unlike autonomy, where we need at least a simple living being, we can start observing stability with non-living objects.

Let's take a cube. If we put it on a table resting on one of its faces, it will be in a stable position. As long as nobody pushes the cube and the table is not tilted or shaken, the cube will stay put. The first thing to notice is that stability depends on the type and characteristics of the object, on its environment, and how they relate to each other. How does it depend on the object? It's easier for a cube to stay stable than it is for a ball. The shape is important. The weight also matters. When shaking the table, a heavier cube is more stable than a lighter one. And speaking of shaking, this is one of the ways stability is challenged by a change in the environment. But the environment has many other ways to influence the stability of an object, both global, such as gravity, and local, such as the surface of the table or what we are going to do next to the cube.

Let's now tilt the cube a bit and then release it. The cube will recover quickly. It will go back to rest on the same face. But if we increase the angle, at some point the cube will tip over and rest on the neighbouring face in the direction of tilting. From one stable state, it will pass through a short unstable one to reach a new stable state.

Bowling pins show similar but more interesting behaviour. They can wobble for a moment and remain upright. Wobbling is a short period of dynamic stability that brings back the initial state of static stability.

If we disturb a ball, it will aim towards a stable position, just like the cube. But unlike the cube, it will get there in a different way. It becomes more interesting when the ball is not on the table directly, but in a bowl. It rests at the lowest point inside the bowl until we push it sideways. When released, the ball won't be in a stable position anymore. The ball will start rolling inside the bowl, getting lower and lower until it finally stops and rests at its stable position at the bottom of the bowl.

There are two things to notice here. Although both the ball and the environment work together to reach a state of equilibrium, we somehow tend to ascribe it solely to the ball. I wrote, "the ball will start rolling". We talk about the ball; the ball is what grabs our attention. It moves when disturbed, while the bowl does nothing. When something is in focus, it tends to use that attention to obscure the role of the environment. And even saying, "it tends to use", endows it with autonomy, evading our responsibility for how we think about it. It seems that languages, at least those originating from Europe, evolved to be object-oriented. The spotlight is on the object, while the context and the observer are cast in shadow. That's another disbalance we need to be aware of.

The second thing to notice is that so far, for both the cube and the ball, the stable position is a position of rest, a position when the object doesn't move in relation to surrounding objects. However, the way we use stability is broader than that.

When flying in a plane, we call the state of the plane stable, although the plane is moving fast. Our feeling of stability changes when we hit turbulence, and that's not related to a perceivable change of speed. The same applies to a ball. If we roll the ball down a smooth chute, that is a sort of stable state, although the ball is not at rest and it is accelerating. Further down, the surface of the chute becomes rough, and the ball bobbles and jumps as it rolls down. We can't call it stable any more. The shape of the chute also influences the stability of rolling. Now the ball meets some sharp curves, and its momentum takes it up the sides of the chute as it negotiates the turns. It looks like it might almost fly off the edge of the chute, but it sways a few times until its rolling stabilizes. After another short straight section, the chute splits into two channels side by side with a rounded ridge between them. The ball rolls up onto and along the ridge in the middle, but it is in an unstable state and it quickly rolls off the ridge down into one of the channels on either side. How quickly the ball rolls off the ridge depends on the width of the ridge and the steepness of the sides of the channels.

Whether we place a cube or a ball on a table, both will stay put when we remove our hand. That won't necessarily be the case with a cone. If we place a cone on its base, it will be even more stable than the cube. But if we put it on its point, it won't stay up long, and will fall. Unless it's a spinning top. When spun, it will remain balanced on its tip due to the angular momentum. It will spin and move on the surface as if dancing, but we still call that dynamic state *stable*.

Both the ball rolling down the chute and the spinning top can be seen as stable even when moving rapidly. Once again, the scale matters. Stability at a certain scale, like seeing the top spinning on its point, is achieved through the right kind of instability at the lower scale. The top remains the same, upright and spinning, by virtue of all its parts being in different positions all the time. Already here, we see that certain kinds of diversity can contribute to stability. It is similar with bowling pins. They can be in a state of dynamic stability when wobbling. That stability is temporary and quickly replaced by a static stability, either after regaining an upright position or after tipping over.

The stability of objects depends on the objects, the way they are situated in their environment, and somebody stating the desired target state. Objects have various relationships with their surroundings, but the internal structures of some can give them special properties regarding stability. Such structures have dynamic relationships that can respond to a disturbance and bring the object back to a stable state from within. For example, when a spring is stretched and then released it will go back to a stable state, a balloon will recover its shape if not squeezed too much, and a roly-poly toy will recover its upright position when tilted.

Playing with cubes, balls, cones, pins, balloons, springs, and roly-polies can teach us a lot about stability. Yet these objects always behave the same way. A cube will behave like a cube every time you play with it. If you take it out of its stable state, it will respond as expected. It won't suddenly start behaving like a cone or a spring. But if we move to a more sophisticated case, that of organisms, they are not as predictable.

For living organisms, stability can refer to their population, their interaction with the environment, the construction of their niche, or the internal state of an individual organism. We'll focus on the latter case. Our interest is in their viability – how they keep living. For an organism to be in a stable, healthy condition, some variables need to be kept within limits. There are regulatory mechanisms that take care of that. For example, human organisms are able to regulate their temperature, levels of sugar, calcium, and iron. They internally keep these variables within certain boundaries. When that ability reaches its limit, the solutions are no longer internal.

They require some action, some interaction with the environment. For example, when it's cold, we go inside or somewhere where it is warm, or we start moving. Sometimes different strategies need to be tried out (diversity comes in here) to bring back that variable into the viable range, and if possible, within the comfort zone. These strategies may use tools and technologies, for example, fire and clothes. Now, when we are cold, we just turn the heating on, or we put on an extra sweater. What's more, the heating is normally regulated so that the temperature inside our houses remains stable even when the temperature outside changes. We can achieve similar regulation with layers of clothes, which was what Ferenc did in the story from the first chapter. In these cases, the diversity (changes in temperature) is eliminated or reduced by some mechanism or by a combination of actions and technology, so that the desired stability is maintained.

Stability is important for organizations as much as it is for organisms. Companies often operate in turbulence. For regular disturbances, they are equipped with structure and processes to deal with them. When an employee leaves, that's a disturbance that triggers some organizational response to restore stability. Such a response could be an instance of a standard recruitment process. Or it could be a decision for a different kind of sourcing. For example, when an accountant leaves, some small and medium-sized companies turn to an accounting service provider.

Organizations are better equipped for small disturbances than for big ones. In fact, many functions and processes for handling small disturbances have been established as standard. The recruitment process is such an example. A more recent case is compliance.

Sometimes the disturbance can be bigger. And it can be of a type experienced in the past, or completely new. When a whole team leaves, that can be a very big shake up. Although it looks like the same type as when one employee leaves, just with bigger magnitude, it is in fact, qualitatively different. For some organizations it may still trigger an instance of the recruitment process, but others may react with structural changes, a different kind of sourcing, or a bigger organizational transformation to prevent other teams leaving.

Big disturbances can destabilize organizations for a long time. Examples of such disturbances are budget cuts in public sector organizations, new regulation with high impact on operations in the private sector, a serious drop in sales due to a new competitor, a loss of production capacity due to a natural disaster, and a countrywide lockdown imposed to slow the spread of a virus. Some organizations invest in forecasting so that they are not taken by surprise. Others invest in preparing their staff to expect the unexpected.

… and Diversity

Organizations as we know them are a recent phenomenon, less than two centuries old. They are a new kind of species inhabiting the planet. Organizations have had some time to learn how to live, how to deal with difficulties and how to survive. But the organizations *of* humans are in any case much younger than organizations *in* humans. The individual humans have certainly had more time to learn, and so there is more to learn *from* them. One such organization is the immune system. Here's how it works.

The Immune System

The body is constantly invaded by microorganisms, such as bacteria and viruses. The microorganisms that cause diseases are called *pathogens*. These pathogens have to be dealt with if the body is to survive and to function well. The cells that fight pathogens are called *lymphocytes.* There are three main types, NK cells, B cells, and T cells. NK stands for Natural Killer cells, and it's obvious what they do. They kill. They know how to kill, but they don't know who to kill. The B cells tell them that. And the role of T cells is to help the B cells. How does this all happen?

On the surface of B cells there are Y-shaped molecules, which serve as receptors. These receptors are called *antibodies.* They can detach from the B cell, flow with the blood, and may encounter similar molecules on the surface of other cells. If the shape of an antibody is similar enough to the shape of another molecule, it binds to it. The better the match, the stronger the binding. Through this binding, the other molecule is "recognized" and if it happens to be harmful, it's marked for destruction.

The main problem for the immune system is dealing with uncertainty. It cannot know in advance what kind of pathogens will invade the body. Thus, it cannot plan and prepare antibodies with the right shape. How does the immune system solve this?

By generating enormous diversity.

The other cells in the body have a low mutation rate, and that is good for the body. Their mutations are treated as errors. For the B cells, it's just the opposite. B cells have the highest mutation rate of all the cells in the human body. It is one million times higher than that of other body cells. It is rightly called *hypermutation.* Through this hypermutation, B cells have diversity, which is needed to try to deal with uncertainty.

Diversity of B cells is the way the immune system can increase the chance of matching the pathogens *type.* To match their *number,* it needs a way to quickly reproduce.

The overall development of B cells goes through two stages. The first one is in the bone marrow where B cells are created. It is the primary lymphoid organ. That's where the high diversity is generated through hypermutation. After they are created, B cells travel with the blood to a secondary lymphoid organ, such as the

> spleen or a lymph node. Here the B cells whose antibodies have a confirmed binding to other molecules, get activated. Once activated, they start to divide, producing copies of themselves. There is some mutation here as well. The newly born antibodies are tested for binding to the pathogen's surface molecules and the better the binding, the more the B cells reproduce. While at the first stage, there is enough diversity of B cells to match the diversity of the invader cells, at this second stage, the matching *quantity* of cells is produced.

The immune system is an organization in which the Stability–Diversity balance is remarkably well maintained. Stability can be seen at several scales. When the stable functioning of the organism is distorted by a disease, it is the immune system that restores stability. It does so by maintaining enormous diversity of B cells. At another scale, while B cells have evolved to have a high mutation rate, so they can be as different as possible, all other cells have evolved to maintain a low mutation rate, to be as similar as possible. And if we zoom out again, the stability of the organism contributes to biodiversity, which in turn keeps the ecosystem stable.

The immune system can handle, with an impressive success rate, one of the most difficult problems organizations face – uncertainty. It doesn't know what will invade the body. Then, when the invading cells are there, some of them are new, some of them have been dealt with previously. The way to match the new invaders is to have diversity. Dealing with known ones requires some kind of memory, so that the old successful responses are reapplied. Maintaining the old responses while generating novel reactions is another level and another way of seeing the balance.

The threats come from pathogens, from various foreign cells invading the body. But B cells, with the help of T cells, simply mark the receptor molecules of certain cells as "bad". Some foreign cells are bad, others are good, and the immune system can make mistakes. It may mark harmless foreign cells as "bad", and such situations we call allergies. But it can also mark the body's own cells as "bad", which is what happens in autoimmune diseases, such as diabetes and lupus. And here's an interesting third case. Some of our own cells are marked as "bad", but not by mistake. Their removal is important for the viability of the organism.

More primitive creatures might not be blessed with such a sophisticated regulatory system in their bodies, but they can be quite successful by regulating collectively. Beehives, for example, have a regulatory mechanism to achieve a stable temperature, based on – guess what – diversity. To us, honeybees look like copies of a single original bee, but in fact, their bodies differ. Bees heat up by buzzing and cool down by fanning their wings. If all bees were the same, when the temperature fell, they'd all start buzzing at the same time, and when it got hot, they'd all start fanning at the same time. That would make the beehive temperature not only unstable, but it would cause it to madly go up and down. Diversity prevents this. Different bees respond to different temperature levels by starting and stopping buzzing and fanning at different times. This way, the beehive not only maintains its internal temperature when the outside temperature changes – it does it gradually.

The benefits of bee diversity don't stop with temperature regulation. Bees also have various strategies for selecting which flowers to collect nectar from. All flowers look similar to bees, but each bloom contains different rewards. By applying diverse strategies, bees achieve a much more stable overall collection of nectar in spite of the variability of the foraging market. A clever way to manage risk.

The importance of diversity to manage risk has been known since ancient times. As with B cells, these kinds of strategies are successful in dealing with uncertainty. And the biggest threat has always been starvation. The unpredictability of food supplies stabilized various practices. It made hunters gather in bands to average out the daily fluctuations in their catch. For nomadic hunter-gatherers, the solution was to move to another location with higher food availability. A third strategy for farmers, and one that appears contrary to the logic of efficiency, is to scatter their plots of land. The most studied example is that of medieval English peasants, but it was practised all over the world. In some parts of Papua New Guinea and Peru, land scattering is still common today.

Such is the case, or was until recently, with the potato farmers in the district of Cuyocuyo in southern Peru. Each household owned a large number of small pieces of land, which they kept scattered over a big area. Most had more than ten and some up to 25. Consolidating these parcels may seem like the most sensible thing to do, but the farmers kept them dispersed. This turned out to be a smart risk strategy. Since their strips were scattered, the risk of various hazards (insect blight, theft, or frost) was spread and the probability of getting something from their land every year was greater. Again, they achieved stability through diversity. Forfeiting a high yield in good years to get something, however meagre, every year is like striking a deal with fortune. Modern practices might be different, but Peruvian farmers must keep doing something right. Today, Peru is the biggest potato producer in Latin America. And they wouldn't do any better if they farmed only high-yield varieties.

If potato farming in Peru was an example of mitigating risk through diversification, 19th century Ireland is an example of the opposite. Relying on potatoes as the main food source was the reason for the heavy food crisis in the mid-1840s, taking one million lives. The potato blight struck many countries in northern Europe but none of them suffered as badly as Ireland, for the other countries had more diverse farming and diets. For example, while potatoes ranged from 2% of arable land in Spain to 14% in Belgium, in Ireland it was 32%. Respectively, the highest daily consumption in continental Europe was 0.5 kilograms per capita in Belgium. In Ireland, it was 2.1 kilograms.

The Stability–Diversity balance can be seen in many human activities, including in art. In music, for example, diversity is produced by using tensions while resolutions restore stability. That's how the balance works at the level of a phrase. At the level of a musical piece, the key, tempo, and the time signature ensure stability, while the variations in the melody, harmony, and loudness bring the diversity.

The plots of plays, movies, and books are diverse, and yet most of them go through the periods of setup, confrontation, and resolution. They are even similar if we zoom in, where popular stories show a sequence of similar stages and turning points. With successful movies, the turning points even happen at the same places in the runtime.

Diversity plays an important role in organizations. Companies diversify their product range, their investment portfolio, and more recently they have started stimulating diversity in the workplace. Take the last example. A company trying to sell to new client groups benefits from diversity in finding ways to reach them. More generally, bringing people from different nationalities, backgrounds, ages, genders, and disabilities increases the chances of solving complex problems by having different perspectives. Again, more than just past experience or current demand should influence the choice. Sometimes the best ideas come from people who aren't a good match with the job profile or have been silent in times of favourable sailing but then come up with unexpected new ideas when there is a storm or no wind. In my experience as an employer, I found out that people who did not have a good fit with the technical requirements or did not fit well in the team, showed unique and much-needed qualities in difficult times. Three such qualities stand out in my memory: perseverance, ingenuity, and loyalty.

Ensuring diversity in the workplace is often motivated by social justice and responding to policies for equal employment opportunities. Workforce diversity – to use the accepted term – is then commonly accepted as something to put up with or something to show off in order to attract socially sensitive clients or appease regulators. If some benefits are realized, then they are regarded as compensation and luck.

The argument here is not related to social justice, without downplaying its importance. Neither does it consider the benefits accidental. Diversity in general, and workforce diversity in particular, actually improves collective intelligence and increases effectiveness and resilience in challenging situations. In other words, diversity should be encouraged and supported, even if you exclude the ethical motive completely. As with B cells in the immune system, the unknown requires a pool of different people, as well as enabling the same people, to come up with different ideas.

Diversity in the office and on the shop floor is just as important as that of the organizational leaders. When board members are of different backgrounds and personalities, that usually produces two effects. One is an increase in disagreement and conflict. The other is increased creativity and higher problem-solving capacity. The size of these effects is also influenced by the amount of time board members spend together and the nature of their interactions. What is commonly overlooked is that surface-level diversity, such as race, gender, and age, is just as important as diversity in background and personality.

It is not only the diversity of people and ideas that matter, but also the diversity of their relationships. Employees tend to maintain social links with their close office mates, or people with whom they communicate frequently due to the nature of their work. Such behaviour is reinforced within functional silos. Silos appear due to a combination of too much autonomy, discussed in the previous chapter, and good maintenance of local stability, which we will analyze later. Other natural factors contribute as well, like homophily – the tendency for people to bond with others who are like them. They might share the same office, department, background, profession, interests, behaviour patterns, beliefs, race, nationality, or social status. This combination of natural forces (homophily) and structural conditions (departments, teams) results in less diverse relationship types within organizations.

Diversity is difficult to achieve, even when some of the corporate constraints are relaxed or when collaboration is enabled by technology. Big organizations implementing collaborative and social network platforms to stimulate, among other things, diversity of relationships, often experience the opposite effect. Their employees tend to recreate the silos from the physical world in the virtual space. Sometimes large parts of the real-world organizational structure are recreated as virtual communities, teams, and channels. As a result, the silos get reinforced, buttressed by another parallel communication channel.

Even if a collaborative platform cannot prevent homophily, it can shift it from work ties to those based on interests. But this potential is limited by the habits reinforced in the history of having predominant relationships inside the organizational unit.

It's easy to see the balance between Stability and Diversity in the evolution of species. A diversity of traits is generated. Some traits are passed on and stabilized through generations, and others disappear. Similar dynamics are observed in emergent organizations, for example, open-source software projects. They are not formally created. They emerge out of interactions between participants, artefacts, and rules. Developers have no formal commitment; they come and go. That brings diversity of skills and ideas. The contributors create code, some of which is stabilized in the next release, and some is abandoned. The same applies to new features. Here, the diversity of users contributes a lot. Through attention, discussions, voting, and other forms of interaction and selection, certain features stabilize. The user interface also tends to stabilize. Its evolution uses various experiences, selecting those which are more commonly used. Open-source projects that don't have enough diversity end up being used by only a few users, do not attract new developers, and quickly die. The other extreme gives similar results. Without a way to stabilize features, the interface, and documentation, an open-source project will not sustain the critical mass of users needed to keep it alive and stimulate further development.

Companies are especially pressed to diversify in competitive markets. They come up with specific products to address a customer group with particular preferences, offer a new combination of products and services, create a niche, or a whole new market. All these ways to differentiate in their environment drive increased internal diversification. Such diversification helps them to adapt to the environment. But it also increases internal complexity. When this is seen as a problem, it is often managed in a way that further increases complexity. We'll see that in more detail later.

When Stability is bad

We associate stability with smooth functioning, health, and comfort. It is generally a good thing. People evolved better ways to maintain stability, both internally (immune system, autoregulation of sugar, calcium, and iron levels) and externally (tools and technologies). Yet, stability can be, and often is, a bad thing.

What is good or bad is a matter of perspective, but going into such philosophical discussion is beyond the objectives of this book and doesn't serve the observational habits it tries to build. That's why we will associate "good" with the notion of health and success, and we'll zoom out when in doubt. What do we mean by *zoom out*? A department may be healthy and successful when measured by getting more budget, growing its staff, and increasing its influence. Yet it may be slowing down the organization it belongs to. Similarly, an organization might be healthy at the expense of community or society.

The phenomena of bad stability can be put in two broad categories, *stability bliss* and *pathological stability*.

Stability bliss

Companies enjoying long periods of stability tend to develop organizational atrophy, hyper-efficiency, and blindness.

Organizational atrophy develops when there are only small disturbances for a long period of time. Responses to restore stability are not trained, and the organization gets out of practice. Similarly, a muscle will get weak when not used, and an organ or limb that is no longer needed will atrophy through generations. Organizations enjoying stability tend to decrease their capabilities to handle negative stimuli.

Stability bliss is not only about inertia and being in a dormant state due to a long period of comfort. It is also a stable pattern of structural decisions for resource allocation. Whatever contributes to stability is maintained, strengthened, and enlarged. And whatever is redundant or not related to maintaining the status quo, is reduced. Interestingly, the reduction of redundant resources and capabilities happens both in a very stable and in a very unstable state. Organizations in a stable state, believing that the stability will last, tend to see less utility in what does not directly contribute to it. Organizations in an unstable state are pressed to cut costs and first cut whatever is not currently and directly important for survival.

Organizational bliss affects innovation and market awareness.

When the current way of doing things works and operations are stable, it is natural to see innovation as a threat. "If it works, don't fix it." After all, innovations are not only distracting and consume resources, they are self-inflicted disturbances. When innovation is woven into the company's culture, which by itself is a desirable state, the practice of innovation can itself become a routine. The target number of innovations is achieved and reported, without trying anything truly new and useful.

And last, we come to organizational blindness. Having a long, calm period, when threats are small or absent, kills the habits of being alert and scanning the horizon. The range of perception narrows and sensitivity weakens. Organizations get short-sighted or even blind. The risk of missing environmental signals increases. They could miss a threat to the current stability or an opportunity for a new type of stability that might last longer.

Some companies combine product research with market research, the logic being that both of these activities look outside the organization and their results are not used now, but potentially in the future. Such a combination of concerns can be productive. But when a company is in a state of stability bliss, it might be easier to marginalize the two functions when they are combined. In any case, the focus on maintaining stability will directly lead to worse conditions for innovation. Even when there is no actual policy and budgetary impact, talented people working in research tend to make career choices that move them closer to the hot topic of the day, and away from their current dormant employer.

Organizational atrophy, hyper-efficiency, and blindness reinforce each other. Hyper-efficiency does not leave capacity for innovation and market awareness, which in turn won't provide justification for maintaining redundant capacity and innovation.

Pathological Stability

Humans create organizations to deal with greater complexity than they could individually. The newly created organization could be a start-up company with an idea for an original product, or it could be a new agency established by the government as a response to a recent problem. Such a new organization (as any other), through various cohesion factors and tools (see Chapter 1, "Autonomy and Cohesion"), by its natural development, reduces the autonomy of its members and increases its own autonomy.

If the initial idea of a start-up company is not successful, and yet the company is established and has some history, it often finds another way to survive based on a new idea. That new idea may have little to do with the initial one. Yet, surviving this way is not pathological.

When a government agency is created to address a particular problem, this is justified if the problem is expected to persist and grow. But even when the problem is solved or just disappears, the agency will try to survive by finding another problem or by keeping the problem alive. The latter is a typical case of pathological stability.

We can also see that phenomenon in companies. A new department or subsidiary is established with a particular function. Even if it starts in a self-organizing mode, when such a sub-organization grows there will be somebody leading it. That leader will gain power. The power is exercised by reducing the range of decisions of those with less power (more about that in the "Productive Paradoxes" chapter). Part of the power is used for making the department effective, but some power is used to stay in power. Sometimes all the power may be used only for that. In a similar way as a leader may use their power and capacity to maintain the status quo, the sub-organization itself, when it has sufficient autonomy, will try to perpetuate itself, even when its original function is no longer needed or relevant for the whole organization. Again, this is pathological stability.

It could be that the department grows, and it finds a way to scale-up its self-organization, so there is nobody in power. That might reduce the risk of pathological stability, but it's not guaranteed. There is always a mechanism to maintain identity and viability, and it might see risks in cooperation. Such is the case when autonomy is allowed, but failure is not supported.

I worked with a company which had very diverse and autonomous divisions. These divisions had quarterly targets and a lot of freedom in how to achieve them. But when there were opportunities to get bigger business by combining their strengths and mutually compensating their weaknesses, some of the divisions evaluated such a cooperation as a high risk. The bigger market, client, or tender has a lower probability of success, for external and internal reasons. The external reasons are obvious: the competition and the overall market uncertainty. The internal reasons are not being in control, combined with weaker cross-divisional coordination when compared to the intra-divisional one. What makes that risk big, is not the lower probability of success alone, but also in combination with the investment and attention needed. By allocating resources for a cross-divisional project, each division has fewer resources to achieve its own independent target. That risk might be perceived as high, even when there is a fair chance for success of the big project, if a division doesn't trust that the revenue will be distributed in proportion to efforts.

A pathological subsidiary can be very resilient. It can be active and inventive to maintain its viability. In fact, when survival is at risk, pathological subsidiaries are able to allocate a lot of resources for self-preservation, as they are not engaged in value-adding activities. Such formations turn into organizational tumours. And they can grow and become more resilient to both internal and external attempts to destroy them.

There is another flavour of pathological stability. It is born with good intentions, as was the case with creating a new government agency. The intention now is to fight organizational silos. To understand this pathology, we have to first see how silos come into being. For that we need to put on the Autonomy–Cohesion glasses.

Silos appear when there is too much autonomy and not enough cohesion. The fragmentation logic is that of division of labour. The division of labour has been the main principle for structuring organizations in the last two centuries. It is still the dominant approach for allocating resources, information, and power in companies and public institutions. The new dynamics in a connected world have revealed a rich spectrum of problems related to these structures ranging from ineffective coordination to turf wars. The reaction was to apply the conventional stigmatizing label, "silo", which led to the birth of a whole industry of silo-fighters armed with silo-bridging or silo-breaking services, methods, and technologies.

The two main strategies, "Bridging the Silos" and "Breaking the Silos", look like the soft and the hard approach, respectively.

The proponents of the first, opt for bridging over breaking, not from having a better understanding of history and context, but due to their insufficient resources and power. Their narrative features a rich repertoire of metaphors, such as walls, chasms, stovepipes, and islands. If their story is sold, they get permission to build – as such a narrative logically suggests – bridges between the silos.

The problem with these bridges is that they are either brittle and quickly break, or they are strong enough to defend their reason to be. They break easily when they stop channelling resources before the patience needed to put up with their initial failures runs out. However, some bridges get to the stage of having a persistent identity, of having a mind of their own. These bridges go from being a temporary measure, managed as a project, into an operation. The silo-bridging operation is now recognized by the organization as an ongoing role and function. If the reason the bridges exist are silos, and the bridges want to keep on bridging, then the silos have to be kept healthy and strong, since they are what the bridges rest upon. This is the second type of pathological stability. Of course, some of the silos that are bridged can be themselves in a state of pathological stability.

The bridges reinforce and perpetuate themselves up to a point when they are recognized as silos in their own right. The problem is often solved by building new bridges between them. In this way, a cancerous fractal of bridges starts to grow.

The other strategy, "Breaking the Silos", can bring its own pathologies but they are not related to the Stability–Diversity balance. In short, the difficulty is that those breaking a silo see it only as a problem and don't analyze what that silo was a solution for. Once the silo is removed, the silo breakers in the organization face unexpected problems, or worse, the outsiders brought in to remove the silo are gone and other people are left to deal with the original issues.

The third form of pathological stability resembles bridging the silos in its attempts to achieve better efficiency. And it is again a case where the cure turns into a parasite, but it has a particular dynamic which is worth studying. The way to do it will be with the next story. It's fictional, but it's created out of common patterns of several real cases.

Dealing with duplication of IT investments

GAPS is a big public sector organization with 18,000 employees. Its main tasks are policy formulation and coordination of policy execution in several domains. There is a separate department for each domain. These departments are very autonomous. In fact, they act as separate organizations. Yet, the budget of GAPS is distributed centrally. There are also common rules and administration policies for human resources, budgeting, and communication across the departments.

Digitalization of core and support processes has been going on for years. Some requirements were met by developing custom software, others by buying off-the-shelf packages. The IT budget has been constantly increasing, in spite of the large number of failed projects. Each department had its own IT unit, and its own IT budget.

At some point, the number of separate software applications in GAPS passed 1,000 and continued to increase. Most of them were bought or built without realizing or ignoring the fact that the functionality needed was already provided by an existing application. Sometimes, when it was clear that certain functionality could be reused, there was always a good justification to avoid reusing it. The real reasons were twofold. Reusing something from another department resulted in, firstly, unpleasant dependency, and secondly, getting behind in the budget spending competition. In the public sector, this competition is intensified by the rule of getting less money next year if the current budget is not used.

There was also too little concern with application integration. When such need became acute, it resulted in new integration projects consuming additional IT budget. Once there was an interface between two applications and they were updated, the interface had to be updated too. The result was ever increasing IT spending and a bigger and more precarious IT landscape.

The situation got messier and more inefficient. That much was clear for years, but it wasn't until the budget cuts started that it was decided to do something about it.

The first thing was to get a common understanding of the problem, by assigning a consulting company to do a study. The consulting company was a good one, but like many others, they use their public sector clients to train their junior consultants in the field. That particular study was no exception. It wasn't carried out very well, not only due to the lack of experience of the field workers but also due to the limited access to information that was allowed. Yet, the final report revealed that the majority of the software applications had duplicated functionalities.

That report was lucky. Unlike other similar reports, it appeared at a time when it provided excellent support for a certain political agenda that involved a serious cost-cutting programme. It gave budget, and thus life, to new project species aiming to rationalize the IT landscape. These projects came with various tools and techniques to discover duplicated investments, to propose solutions to the current situation, and changes to avoid it in the future. Some initiatives resulted in huge documentation efforts, others supported cross-department programmes for taking decisions on the automation of common processes. Subsequently, the IT budget was increased. Apart from pure IT projects, the IT budget was now also financing IT rationalization projects.

Some of them were actually successful, but their success made them part of a new pathological symbiosis. As their mandate was only in IT, the budgeting and procurement processes and rules remained intact. They continued to produce new inefficiencies and to fund IT rationalization projects aiming to reveal and reduce these inefficiencies after the fact. The GAPS IT rationalization unit entered a new state of pathological stability. Certain IT rationalization methods failed and were replaced by others, and new ones always succeeded in distracting attention from the bigger problem. But even when it was understood, the mandate for IT rationalization was always too low in the food chain to have any influence at the corporate level.

The story of GAPS is probably familiar to many of you. I saw variations of it in both public and private organizations. I saw it in financial, insurance, telecommunications, and utility companies, but it is not specific to them. It is a story rich with organizational lessons, yet it is told here to showcase one particular kind of pathological stability. As with the pathology of bridging the silos, it starts with good intentions to heal the organization from a serious disease that is impeding its functions and progress and, in some cases, even threatening its viability. Then it ends up in a new stable symbiosis, where there is less chance of drawing attention to the problem, for it looks like it's already been taken care of.

This chapter is about Diversity–Stability, but twice already we have used the Autonomy–Cohesion glasses in combination. Now, we are going to put them on for a third time.

In the previous chapter we discussed the oscillation between decentralization and centralization. There was the example that after a stage of inefficiencies and duplication of IT investments, similar to that in GAPS, many organizations opt for centralization. In the case of IT, this typically means one data centre for the whole organization, selecting the best out of similar applications and making it a corporate service, establishing tighter IT governance, and so on.

Such centralization, however, greatly reduces the autonomy of the sub-organizations. It typically results in higher cost, slower processes, reduced adaptive capacity, and lower service quality. This comes from looking at the problem in isolation. For example, if one sub-organization developed an excellent application which was selected as the best and it was decided to make it a corporate service, this service would need a service provider, ensuring availability, scalability, and quality. How is this handled?

One popular solution is to turn the in-house development team into a corporate service provider. I have yet to see that work. A team that is a good software developer, cannot also be expected to be a good service provider.

Sometimes becoming an internal service provider doesn't work because the whole department is not able to handle its dual role in the inter-organizational market. It experiences identity dissonance. The development team belongs to a department providing a core service, and that department should now also provide a support service, which is what an IT service is in any non-IT organization.

Another popular solution is to transfer the service to the corporate IT provider. Such a scenario may work for assuring service availability and scalability, but less so for service quality. It's not likely that the new host of the application will provide the combination of relationships, skill, vision, and culture that made the application successful where it was born and initially developed.

And finally, we again have the problem of reduced autonomy. If GAPS had executed a centralized policy to solve the IT rationalization problem, it would have resulted in departments getting much less value from their IT investments, which wouldn't correspond so well to their particular needs, cycles, and culture.

This was an example of looking at a situation with both Stability–Diversity and Autonomy–Cohesion glasses. It becomes clear that stability is somehow related to cohesion, and autonomy to diversity.

Coming back to the pathological stability, let's summarize. We have identified three types of pathological stability. The first is the phenomenon of a sub-organization becoming concerned solely with its own survival and growth, regardless of what this brings to the organization it belongs to. The second is the bridges between silos actually strengthening the silos and becoming silos themselves. And the third is an initiative to deal with inefficiencies, being constantly fed with new inefficiencies, due to its scope of action and financing model. There are other types of pathological stability, but these three should suffice to increase awareness when things are going in the wrong direction.

When is Diversity bad?

Maintaining a high level of diversity is important, yet if other factors are not considered, it may have a negative effect. Diversity alone is not sufficient.

Diverse teams with members lacking cognitive flexibility and trust perform worse than homogeneous groups. That's at the team scale. At an organizational scale, internal diversification leads to high levels of internal complexity, which in turn causes conflict and instability. That second case of diversity producing negative effects at the organizational scale is more common and has bigger consequences. Let's take a closer look at it to answer the following questions. Why do organizations increase their internal diversity? Which are the popular types of drivers? How do the issues with internal complexity arise? What new problems and dilemmas are caused by the popular ways of dealing with increased internal complexity?

Organizations are constantly challenged by their environment. Something changes or threatens them directly, and they need to respond in a way that can assure at least their continuity, at best their prosperity. As seen earlier, these changes and threats are what organizations adapt to so that they can restore stability. They often do it by increasing their diversity. But if done mechanically and myopically, then the increased diversity itself makes the organizations unstable. How does this happen?

There are different kinds of changes in the environment. The following three frequently drive internal diversification: change in the regulations that the organization has to comply with; increased competition that threatens market share and profits; and new technology.

Compliance

Market regulation has increased in the last two decades. There have been lots of legislation changes, some with smaller impacts applicable to specific sectors, others affecting organizations globally. Two prominent, recent examples of legislation changes with global impact are the Sarbanes–Oxley (SOX) Act of 2002 and the General Data Protection Regulation (GDPR) of 2016.

The organizational reaction to a regulatory change might initially be a small one. The topic makes it onto the board agenda, and the board decides to establish a temporary task force. If not a task force, then at least they assign an ongoing responsibility to somebody. That new compliance role typically appears in the legal, accounting, internal audit, or quality assurance unit. It starts small. Just another responsibility assigned to somebody. It might be temporary, and then often it turns into a permanent position. That requires additional training and specialization. Quite often, somebody who is already specialized is hired from outside to take care of the compliance issue. Whatever the source, the result is that one or more existing organizational units are internally diversified with a new role or position. This diversity grows with the increased size and frequency of compliance disturbances. Soon, not just a different focus and skills are required, but also greater capacity. At some point, setting up a separate compliance unit is justified. While initially, the increased diversity is only within a couple of organizational units, it now diversifies the formal organizational structure. That structural change leads to redistribution of budget and power, new cross-unit relationships, and additional coordination challenges.

This is, of course, a simplified description of such a dynamic. In reality, the whole ecosystem is changed in a way such that it influences, and is influenced by, the organizational reaction to the legislation changes. The efforts to organize compliance in a more beneficial way drive synergetic efforts to improve business processes, governance, and overall risk management. Then professional organizations start to form, training and consulting companies extend their portfolio of services, universities bring their curricula up to date, and software providers come up with applications to support the new activity. A whole new discipline called *Governance, risk management, and compliance* (GRC) is born, with its terminology, frameworks, and best practices. It is not the legislation alone, but all these changes that influence the internal diversification in organizations.

Competition

The most common and prominent type of change is when the market changes in a way that decreases, or threatens to decrease, the market share or profits of a company. The list of all types of reactions historically driven by this is huge. And companies invent new ways every day, some of them radically different. For our purposes, it's enough to pick up a few popular ones.

A company may come up with a new product addressing an existing or newly created need. It may offer a service to a customer group not targeted before. This might be just constructing a small niche, or creating a whole new market, as was the case with Airbnb, Uber, and Apple's iTunes. The differentiation might be manifested only as increased sensitivity within an existing customer group. This is the case with so-called Usage-Based Insurance. In one of its varieties, it serves an existing target group of young drivers. Typically, they have high premiums and low no-claims bonuses. An insurer introducing a technology to detect driving patterns differentiates between careful and reckless young drivers, and changes its rules for calculating premiums and bonuses, thus attracting careful young drivers. This, of course, makes other insurers do the same or find even better ways of distinguishing driving patterns within the same target group.

All these cases, targeting a new group of customers, differentiating within an existing one, or creating a new niche or market, are about external differentiation, which will drive higher internal diversity. A bank creates a separate account manager or unit for a particular new client group; a new product development group is separated out and given autonomy outside the Research and Development department; a producer of dental equipment reorganizes to address the need of only senior consumers, and so on. In various ways, competition increases the internal company diversity. Before seeing how this becomes a problem, let's look at the third case.

New technology trend

A third driver is when there is a new trend, especially a technology trend. In some characteristics it resembles the compliance driver, in others, competition. It resembles compliance in the way it creates disciplines, communities, certification programmes, and software services. And it resembles competition, because some companies' successful use of a new technology that helped them increase their market share, presses competitors to catch on. Again, it is the whole ecosystem that is changing. The choices of the adopters, their customers, and the technology vendors influence each other.

Important players in this game are market research companies such as Gartner and Forrester. Often their influence is not due to their predictive capabilities, but due to the market influence they already have. It drives choices that turn some of their predicted changes into self-fulfilling prophecies.

The list of technology trends that changed many organizations and created new ecosystems is long. If, as with compliance, we look at the last two decades, we see that, for example, Business Process

Management (BPM) and Service-Oriented Architecture (SOA) changed markets dramatically, and this is now happening with the Internet of Things (IoT), Machine Learning, Virtual and Augmented Reality, and Robotic Process Automation (RPA), to name just a few. The labels themselves have become buzzwords and have their own life, often creating myths and misconceptions, always feeding and being amplified by social media, itself an ecosystem grown with the help of new technologies.

These technology trends are not developed in isolation. For example, BPM and SOA have influenced and keep influencing each other. More recently, it's a whole cluster of trends around data: Big Data, Analytics, Machine Learning and its umbrella term, Artificial Intelligence (which funnily, is often classified as technology, although it's a research area, and as new, although it's 60 years old). Like compliance, but – in case of Data – faster, wider, and deeper, it changes organizations and creates professions, communities, certification programmes, services, and of course, software products.

Take, for example, the new breed of data scientists. The demand for them grows, and with that, training companies add new courses and universities create new faculties. Of course, a closer look at them would reveal that Data Science is just the new name of the old Faculty of Statistics, or a merger between that and an Artificial Intelligence (AI) research group from Computer Science. In any case, all these changes drive organizations to come up with new positions, such as Chief Data Officer (CDO). In that particular case, it is a natural drift, working together with that new trend, to make such a position acceptable. The traditional Chief Information Officer (CIO) was supposed to be responsible for *information* management. But most CIOs acted instead as Chief Technology Officers or Chief Application Officers who shaped technology choices, architecture decisions, and IT investments. That's an interesting topic by itself, but the point here is only that CDOs, data scientists, data analysts, and other positions appeared in organizations, thus diversifying them. Again, as with compliance and competition, it brought internal diversification at the organizational unit and other levels.

These three drivers can act independently and in combination. The example of Usage-Based Insurance is a mix of competitive pressure and technology trend (IoT). But as it's quite invasive and involves gathering personal data, it requires compliance with the respective regulation (GDPR).

Regulatory compliance, competition, and new technology trends increase internal diversification in organizations. In the beginning, it is a healthy diversification. Organizations match the external variety with internal variety, which will be examined further in the "Stimuli and Responses" chapter. Indeed, that is one of the ways to deal with such environmental stimuli, but there is a danger that even at this stage, diversification might not work if it's done mechanistically.

It looks like this. There is a problem, new regulation (say GDPR), or increased competition. To the latter the answer is to focus on a target group, say Senior Customers, and to catch up with competitors that are successfully using Artificial Intelligence. Then many organizations would appoint a GDPR compliance officer, new account manager for Senior Customers, hire a few data scientists led by a newly appointed AI officer. They see the environmental disturbances as three labelled boxes, and they answer by internally creating three boxes with matching labels. They assign responsibilities and allocate budgets. And that's it; the problem is taken care of. When that's the way to answer environmental changes, diversification won't work, even at this stage.

For those organizations that have sufficient maturity to first better understand the situation and then design the responses, enabling their learning and adaptation, the internal diversification will initially work. But slowly and surely it will increase the internal complexity and the adaptation pressure on all sub-organizations – organizational units, people, and coordination. Then there will be more disagreement, and more and different needs to be met. More communication channels will be needed, and greater coherence due to a redistribution of power to multiple centres with little alignment. All of that is very challenging.

Organizational units and people now need to adapt to changes in both the external and internal environment. The patterns of internal adaptation are similar to the external ones. The coordination and alignment problems are addressed with new coordination structures, responsibilities, and rules. All this costs money, so efficiency goes down. That is the first problem. The second, and the bigger one, is that those new structures, responsibilities, and rules, designed to manage internal complexity, do just the opposite. They increase complexity as there are new entities to be maintained and new relationships between more elements than before.

Unfortunately, when issues accumulate, they often trigger crude cohesion measures. Typically, these include new rules and centralization. The new rules suffocate innovation. The centralization reduces the autonomy of sub-organizations, which actually was the reason the internal diversification was beneficial in the first place.

This is not just a problem of too much diversity. Using both the Stability–Diversity and Autonomy–Cohesion glasses reveals a dependence between internal and external adaptation. Internal diversification could make an organization more successful as it quickly adapts to the external environment. But it brings more internal disagreement and leads to crises of increased internal complexity. Popular solutions to control higher levels of disagreement can be seen as successful internal adaptation, but it is at the expense of the capacity to adapt to the external environment.

Technology trends trigger internal diversification and organizations change. But often – especially when it is technology-induced – they copy models of change and become more alike. When the internal diversification is carried out in a similar way, it brings external homogenization.

Summary

Organizations need to maintain both sameness and otherness. Failing that, they might work for a while, but only in easy times.

With Stability–Diversity glasses we can see stability as stable performance, which is good, but also as doing things the same way, which might not be good, or as pathological stability, which is good at its own level, but parasitic or even cancerous when we zoom out. The same pair of glasses reveals diversity when it appears in different guises – as instability, change, innovation, or disruption, along with the more common team diversity or risk diversification.

Stability and diversity can have more complicated relationships. Maintaining diversity in times of stability can restore stability in times of disturbance. The reason for that is simple: when the next challenge is unknown and unusual, the bigger the repertoire of responses or generators of responses, the greater the chance some of them will be fit for the challenge.

Stability can be observed in objects when they stay put, move, spin, or wobble. It can also be observed in organisms, machines, and organizations. Stability in organizations is dynamic. If compared to objects, it's more like a top spinning or a bowling pin wobbling, only much more complex than that, of course.

Organizations are equipped with various routine mechanisms to restore stability when disturbed. Disturbances can be small, such as a valuable employee leaving, a drop in sales, or an accident in a factory. But they can be big, such as losing a whole market due to new technology, an overall blow from a financial crisis, or a natural disaster. For small disturbances, organizations are equipped with routine mechanisms to restore stability, but for big, and especially for unexpected jolts, they depend on their ability to maintain diversity.

Maintaining stability is not always healthy. Stability can even be very bad for organizations. Such is the case with organizational bliss and pathological stability.

Stability bliss happens when organizations ossify during a long, calm period. It manifests itself as organizational atrophy (responses get out of practice), hyper-efficiency (cutting healthy redundancy), and blindness (no longer scanning the horizon for threats and opportunities).

Pathological stability is when a department or a government agency protects their stability and growth for the sake of it, without bringing value to the bigger organization or network they belong to. Some attempts to bridge organizational silos are also prone to pathological stability.

When expensive waste is created and then its reduction is financed as a project, it often turns into an operation that is in symbiosis with the continued production of more waste. And that's yet another type of pathological stability.

Diversity in organizations is often talked about in terms of workforce diversity. The focus on workforce diversity only addresses surface-level diversity (age, gender, race, and disability), and ignores deep-level diversity (background, personality, attitude etc.). Such a focus also excludes the diversity of ideas, relationships, and innovation, which are treated as something unrelated to diversity.

The other problem is that diversity in organizations is addressed only from an ethical perspective, ignoring or downplaying the evolutionary role of diversity as the only way to deal with uncertainty.

Apart from giving a wider and deeper perspective on diversity, using Stability–Diversity glasses can help protect diversity from natural forces, such as homophily, and from structural conditions, such as departments, projects, and other silos.

But like stability, diversity can also be bad for organizations. That is rarely the case with team diversity or board diversity, but often happens when organizations diversify internally as a response to a new regulation, a new competitor, or new technology.

The Stability–Diversity glasses can help you to see different types of stability and diversity. They can also be useful to see which types of diversity can help or harm stability, and which types of stability can help or harm organizations.

The Stability–Diversity glasses are very useful on their own, but even more so when used in combination with Autonomy–Cohesion glasses.

NOTES

1. And the key to understanding it is exactly in these two words: *different* and *same*.

Using same and different, Stability–Diversity can be presented in a way that both syntactically and semantically looks more like a balance:

Homeostasis–Heterostasis

The word homeostasis comes from the Greek ὅμοιος *homoios*, "similar" and στάσις *stasis*, "standing still", to suggest the idea of "staying the same". *Hetero-* comes from ἕτερος [*héteros*], "another", and is often used as a prefix meaning "different".

With this in mind, Stability–Diversity is the ability to "maintain sameness" balanced with the ability to "maintain difference".

2. The concepts of stability and diversity operate in different dimensions.

I use "operate" for something that is observed and described with stability and diversity as if they do something. For the usage of this pair of glasses, the habit of seeing stability and diversity as having autonomy, as actually doing something, is encouraged.

3. [Exnovation] is an actual strategy for some healthcare practices.

Exnovation was first defined by John Kimberly in 1981 as "removal of innovation from an organisation" (Kimberly, 1981). It became widespread in healthcare. Rodriguez et al. clarify that exnovation removes only innovations "that do not improve organizational performance, are too disruptive to routine operations, or do not fit well with the existing organizational strategy, incentives, structure, and/or culture" (Rodriguez, Henke, Bibi, & Shortell, 2016). While there are positive effects of exnovation in healthcare, such as preventing the "change fatigue" and ensuring that innovations are implemented only when there is adoption capacity and good fit, exnovation can also prevent the adoption of new practices with proven effectiveness. For example, some chronic care management processes with strong evidence for diabetes and depression were not adopted by one-third of the studied practices (ibid.).

4. [T]he analogue for Diversity in *space* is to look at it as a balance itself. This will reveal the second hidden balance, Diversity–Homogeneity.

We looked at Diversity in itself as a balance and still Stability re-entered this balance as Homogeneity.

5. And even saying, "it tends to use", endows it with autonomy, evading our responsibility for how we think about it.

Heinz von Foerster put it brilliantly:

> *Objectivity is a subject's delusion that observing can be done without him. Involving objectivity is abrogating responsibility – hence its popularity.* (Bernhard, 2013)

6. One such organization is the immune system. Here's how it works.

It is now commonly accepted that there is an adaptive immune system and an innate immune system in vertebrates. The story about the immune system is, in fact, only about the adaptive immune system, and more specifically that of humans, which is similar to that of other mammals.

The story itself is a simplified description of the most popular theory of the adaptive immune system. Now, what is a *theory* and why have I chosen *this* one?

> *We human beings propose theories as systems of explanation of what we distinguish as happening in what we observe or do in the realization of our living. Theories are systems of logical deductions that we propose in order to follow the consequences that would arise in a particular situation if we transformed everything in it around the conservation of some set of basic premises that we choose to adopt – either because we accept their validity according to some logical argument or, a priori, because we like them.* (Maturana, 2015)

Based on that, my preference for an explanation on how the adaptive immune system works is in the direction pointed by Francisco Varela and Antonio Coutinho (Varela & Coutinho, 1991).

One of the unresolved problems of immunology is the so-called self/nonself problem, or how the immune system distinguishes own and harmless from foreign and harmful cells. According to Varela, the problem is badly formulated, as the immune system can only "know" itself. It is not driven by antigens. Nor does it have any identity at the cell level. The identity is an emergent property of the operationally closed immune network. Its reactions are not determined by distinguishing own from foreign, and then harmful from harmless. It tries to preserve its identity in a process called self-assertion. What it reacts to is threats to its state. These threats can come from both foreign and own cells. The self-assertion controls the concentration of antibodies and the recruitment of new B cells.

Although I have a preference for this explanation, the story in the chapter describes the mainstream theory. One reason to do so is that the actual divergence in the explanation comes from the solution of the self/nonself problem, which is not treated in the story of the B cells. The second is, no matter which of the two explanations are chosen, the Stability–Diversity balance applies equally.

7. If the shape of an antibody is similar enough to the shape of molecule, it binds to it.

In fact, it is not the whole antibody molecule but only a region of it, called a *paratope*. Accordingly, it binds to a region of the other molecule, called an *epitope*.

8. The first one is in the bone marrow where B cells are created.

This is only the case for mammals. In birds, B cells mature in a lymphoid organ, called "bursa of Fabricius" (Cooper, 2015). The "B" in B cells comes from there and not from bone marrow.

9. This way, the beehive not only maintains its internal temperature when the outside temperature changes – it does it gradually.

To some extent, they can also regulate the humidity of the beehive (Human, Nicolson, & Dietemann, 2006).

10. Bees also have various strategies for selecting which flowers to collect nectar from.

Burns and Dyer have shown that "behavioural variability acts to decrease variation in resource acquisition in the wild" (Burns & Dyer, 2008).

11. A third strategy for farmers, and one that appears contrary to the logic of efficiency, is to scatter their plots of land.

There are other strategies to minimize the risk of starvation, such as buffering (Diamond, 2012). What the three mentioned have in common, is that they rely on diversity to deal with fluctuations and uncertainty. Using a more generic pair of glasses will show that, from another perspective, these strategies have a lot in common with buffering. Such a pair of glasses is introduced in the "Stimuli and Responses" chapter.

12. Such is the case, or was until recently, with the potato farmers in the district of Cuyocuyo in southern Peru.

Farming practices in Cuyocuyo were extensively researched by Carol Goland in the 1980s (Goland, 1993). In the communities studied, each household owned between nine and 26 fields. The farmers grew mainly potatoes but also oca and broad beans. Goland proved that although the farming was labour intensive already, adding the additional cost of working on dispersed plots did not outweigh the benefits of getting sufficient yield each year, regardless of the unpredictability of the agricultural hazards.

13. And they wouldn't do better if they farmed only high-yield varieties.

High-yield potato varieties were introduced in Peru, but Peruvian farmers kept most of the native varieties, which prevented the erosion of biological diversity (Brush, Taylor, & Bellon, 1992).

14. [W]hile potatoes ranged from 2% of arable land in Spain to 14% in Belgium, in Ireland it was 32%.

The source of potato consumption data is Vanhaute et al. (2006).

15. With successful movies, the turning points even happen at the same places in the runtime.

According to Michael Hauge's "Six-stage Plot Structure", successful movie plots go through six stages: Setup; New Situation; Progress, Complications and Higher Stakes; Final Push; and Aftermath and show five similar turning points: Opportunity; Change of Plans; Point of No Return; Major Setback; and Climax. Moreover, in successful movies, these turning points happen at the same percentage of the playtime, the Opportunity around 10%, Change of Plans around 25%, and so on (Hauge, 2018).

16. [Diversity] actually improves collective intelligence.

But it is threatened by conformity, groupthink, and market-based incentive systems (Mann & Helbing, 2016). The minority needs to be rewarded for showing accuracy when the majority opinion has been in error (ibid.).

17. When board members are of different backgrounds and personalities, that usually produces two effects.

Studies on the relationship between board member diversity and performance show mixed results. That by itself, is another confirmation of the balance. Compatibility and diversity are equally important. Yet, most of these studies focus on surface-level diversity (gender, age, and race). A more recent study, using a sample of 385 Norwegian companies, focused on deep-level diversity, including background, abilities, skills, values, attitudes, beliefs, and personality (Torchia, Calabrò, & Morner, 2015). As such, diversity is only perceivable when board members work together for an extended period of time (Harrison, Price, & Florey, 2002). Torchia et al. also studied the influence of the board interactions. They showed evidence of a positive relationship between deep-level diversity and both cognitive conflict (disagreement about the content of the tasks performed) and creativity. In addition, such a relationship is influenced by the team interactions and mediators. A mediator can make the relationship with cognitive conflict disappear, but can also reduce the positive effect on creativity.

18. Similar dynamics are observed in emergent organizations, for example, open-source software projects.

Studying open-source software projects, Lanzara and Morner found out that "the contradictory requirements of innovation and stability in project-based knowledge making are balanced by mechanisms of variation, selection, and stabilization" (Lanzara & Morner, 2003).

19. And they can grow and become more resilient to both internal and external attempts to destroy them.

The mutation rate in cells is slowly evolving and only through generations. At least this was the general understanding until a recent discovery showed that cells can change their mutation rate under stress. They can increase their mutation rate rapidly to adapt to the threat (high ethanol in this case) and when adapted, decrease it (Swings, et al., 2017). These findings help to explain antibiotic resistance in microbes and cancer relapses after chemotherapy. But more generally, they also show that adaptability is underestimated.

20. The other strategy, "Breaking the Silos", can bring its own pathologies but they are not related to the Stability–Diversity balance.

In contrast to silo-bridging, the silo-breaking strategies want nothing less than the destruction of silos. There, the silos are seen only as a problem. Nobody asks what kind of problems this problem was a solution to. Instead, this type of silo-fighter starts waging exhausting wars. These wars can end in several ways. A common one is resource depletion. Another is with the silos withstanding, or with the silo-fighter being chased away or transformed. And then, of course, there could be a victory for the silo-fighters. And this is when the disaster strikes. Having brought the silos down, the silo-fighters are faced with all the problems that were continuously solved by the silos during their lifespan. Usually, they have no preparation to deal with those problems nor the time to come up with and build alternative structures.

21. Diverse teams with members lacking cognitive flexibility and trust perform worse than homogeneous groups.

Some studies show that homogeneous groups perform better compared with heterogeneous groups that lack cognitive flexibility and trust (Roy & Dugal, 1998). Although the samples are not representative, and the authors have not studied performance in situations with high uncertainty where diversity pays off the most, the conclusion about the importance of cognitive flexibility is worth considering. In other words, bringing together people of different race, age, gender, and personality could work when they are open to explore different views and challenge their beliefs.

22. When the internal diversification is carried out in a similar way, it brings external homogenization.

Market research confirms this finding. In their report "The Cost of Losing Creativity" from 2019, Forrester observed that "similar customer experience solutions and heavy investments in common technology platforms create a sea of digital sameness" (Forrester Research, 2019). An important contributor to the similar customer experience is the mass adoption of the same methods and practices. For example, so-called "digitalization" stimulated the adoption of Design Thinking, which despite of proclaiming flexibility, instilled similar approaches in many organizations. Within Design Thinking itself, customer experience techniques, such as the usage of "personas" (Price, 2018) further decreased the sensitivity to consumer diversity and – as a result – the diversity of the created customer experience.

23. [I]gnoring or downplaying the evolutionary role of diversity as the only way to deal with uncertainty.

Fungi, one of the oldest living organisms on the planet, are also currently the most diverse. There are between 2.2 and 3.8 million species (Hawksworth & Lücking, 2017). But what is truly amazing is that they have also diversified their metabolism and methods of reproduction. A recent book by Merlin Sheldrake (Sheldrake, 2020) reveals a lot of little-known facts about fungi.

3

EXPLORATION AND EXPLOITATION

Adaptive systems that engage in exploration to the exclusion of exploitation are likely to find that they suffer the costs of experimentation without gaining many of its benefits. They exhibit too many undeveloped new ideas and too little distinctive competence. Conversely, systems that engage in exploitation to the exclusion of exploration are likely to find themselves trapped in suboptimal stable equilibria. As a result, maintaining an appropriate balance between exploration and exploitation is a primary factor in system survival and prosperity.

— James March

I love going to jazz festivals. Listening to good jazz at home is a pleasure, but what's missing are the vibes during a live performance. And it's not the same when you listen to a recording of a concert. Everything changes when you are actually there, immersed, experiencing directly with all your senses. I guess it's similar with other types of music. But what makes the difference between listening to a recording and being at concert even bigger for jazz, is that it is all about improvisation. And then the experience of single concerts versus festivals is also different. With concerts, you immerse yourself for a couple of hours into a world of magic and then go back to the normal world. But with jazz festivals, you relocate to live in a music village for a couple of days. This doesn't only make it a different experience, but also calls for different kinds of decisions.

Previously, when I learned of a new jazz festival or read the line-up of a familiar one, the way I decided whether to go was simple. I just checked who would be performing. If there were musicians that I liked, but hadn't watched live, or some that I had, but wanted to see again, then I went. If not, I usually wouldn't risk it.

Once I chose to go, this brought more things to consider. Jazz festivals usually have many stages, with parallel performances during the day and into the night. Last time I went to the North Sea Jazz Festival, there were over 80 performances in only a few days. So, there is a good chance that some of those you want to watch will clash, and you are forced to choose. And I kept applying the same low-risk strategy for choosing what to watch as I did for deciding if I should go at all.

Then one day, I arrived late to a festival just before two clashing sets were about to begin. I dashed into the closest hall with no clue as to what I would find. And there I experienced what turned out to be the best concert of the whole festival. I hadn't heard of the group, and if I had read the description beforehand, I would have avoided their performance.

I realized then, that by only choosing concerts with familiar musicians, I was over-exploiting and under-exploring. My strategy was depriving me of learning opportunities and reducing the overall value I got from the festivals.

What happened at that festival changed the way I decide whether to go and which performances to see. Now I not only attend many more concerts of musicians previously unknown to me, but not having a familiar name in the line-up does not determine the decision to buy tickets.

However, when the whole line-up of the festival is completely unknown, then going is all exploration. That's highly risky. When there are no familiar musicians, I listen to recordings of previous concerts of some of the groups. If I like at least two of them, then I usually go to the festival, and once there, I will still check out a few acts I don't know. That's another way to balance exploitation and exploration.

When I am in control, "I restrict the world to what I can imagine or permit", writes Ranulph Glanville. He gives the example of going to a restaurant with friends. If it's always him who chooses the restaurant, the group will only go to the restaurants that he knows. They are limited to his taste and knowledge, or rather – as he admits – by his ignorance. Letting go of control by letting others choose, not only expands his knowledge but would often give a better experience for everyone.

Having the wrong strategy when it comes to jazz festivals and restaurants reduces the pleasure, but in these examples, the decisions make such a small impact that they may not show how important this balance is. Yet, we make similar choices all the time. For example, you might decide to invest your time in getting better at what you currently do well while not allocating time to trying out new things. This may put you in a very unpleasant situation in times when there is no more demand for what you are skilled at, or when you need a change but have difficulty choosing because you haven't tested many alternatives.

Throughout our lives, many of us realize that when making choices, we should have a balance of exploration and exploitation. We should let go of some control and not limit ourselves to what we already know. And that's an important first step, but it's not enough. It takes a greater effort to keep this awareness awake. And somehow, it's also easier at a personal level. How so?

We live our lives and are experiencing every minute of every day. We absorb sounds, tastes, smells, and light and feel the air on our skin. Through evolution we are well equipped to receive a signal when there is even a small problem. We get a scratch and react right away. That's not the case with organizations. They might be missing a whole limb or – and here the metaphor will fail to produce a feeling of exaggeration – a head, without noticing for years. And even if we have learned how to balance exploitation and exploration in our lives, the chances are we are working in organizations that haven't. It's not easy even to imagine what maintaining this balance means for an organization. We can't really step into the shoes of one. What we can do instead is study this phenomenon a little closer, try to understand it better, and then, armed with a new pair of glasses, make the best of that knowledge while we keep learning from what happens. Let's start this study – as it is now customary in this book – with a simpler organization, where it is easier to observe the balance.

Pheromone Trails

Ants move randomly. Well, not all the time. They have ways to direct their movement and behaviour. One way is through pheromones, a kind of chemical they use for communication. It has a vital role when they gather food.

An ant rambles until it stumbles upon a food source. After that its behaviour looks purposeful. It gets a piece of food and brings it back to the nest, leaving a pheromone trail behind. If another ant crosses the pheromone trail, it tends to follow it. When a second ant reaches the food, it takes a piece and carries it to the nest. While it carries the food, that ant also leaves pheromones behind, reinforcing the trail and increasing the chance of other ants finding the food by following the trail.

> Now, imagine three ant colonies. They evolved in such a way that the quality of the pheromone they produce is different. More particularly, in each colony it takes a different time for a pheromone trail to evaporate. The ants in the first ant colony produce pheromone trails that evaporate very quickly. As a result, fewer ants reach the food source and it takes more time to gather the food. There is also the risk that they reach the food spot after the food has already been taken by competitors. In any case, with fast-evaporating pheromone trails, there are many ants rambling with some chance of discovering new food sources. At the same time, there are not enough ants exploiting already discovered piles of food.
>
> The pheromone trails produced by the ants in the second ant colony take more time to evaporate. Compared with the first colony, more ants follow and reinforce them. The second ant colony will be more efficient in foraging. It will have a higher chance of survival.
>
> The ants from the third colony produce pheromones that never evaporate. So even if there are no ants refreshing a pheromone trail, whenever an ant crosses it, the trail is still there and can be followed. The communication role of the pheromone will be very effective. Compared with the other two colonies, more ants from this one will know about the discovered food source and be on their way to collect it. However, the survival chances of the third colony are the worst of the three. There will be many ants exploiting the food sources they find, and they'll keep going to them even after the food is gone. At the same time, there won't be enough ants exploring the territory for new food.

Balancing exploration and exploitation is as vital for the survival of ant colonies as it is for other organizations. Like we did with previous balances, we need to expand the understanding of exploitation and exploration, see it in different contexts, in different kinds of organizations, and at different scales. The objective is to reinforce the pattern so that the glasses start to work. Then exploring the diversity of its manifestations will sharpen your skills for organizational diagnosis and design.

We'll start with the problem of resource allocation, which is the most common understanding of the balance. From this perspective, it is an optimization dilemma. Then, we'll expand the notion of the balance and review a few counterintuitive findings in organizations. Before moving to more complex situations, we'll need some cues and calibration for recognizing exploration – it is far better hidden in the business language than exploitation. Once this calibration is done, we'll be ready to move on to study the more complex dynamics of exploration and exploitation in space and time.

This journey will confirm that imbalances are usually towards over-exploitation. Then the chance is, we will often need to support exploration. But it can't be forced or even managed. At best, it can be enabled. And this not being a book of recipes and advice (as explained in the Introduction), the focus will be on understanding what enabling exploration means and what it takes. Central to this will be recognizing and using the relationship between exploration and constraints.

Lastly, we'll use the new pair of glasses to look at ourselves wearing other pairs, those of the other two balances. That's an advanced exercise, but it won't be too difficult when approached step by step. We've made the first steps already. The next one is the dilemma of resource allocation.

Allocation of resources

You have discovered a gold deposit. How do you allocate your limited resources? How much should you invest in exploiting the deposit you have versus the amount spent on looking for new deposits? You don't know how big the vein is and the amount of gold you can extract from the current mine and you also don't know if you'll find a new one. If you put all your efforts and resources in exploiting the current deposit, you might not have sufficient resources left to look for new ones when this one is exhausted. But the next one you find might be bigger or have higher quality. Yet it is just as likely that you invest a lot in exploring and you don't find another deposit at all, so unlike in exploitation, all that resource will be wasted.

Companies face this dilemma all the time. For example, when there are a few successful markets (clients, consumer groups, or regions), should the company come up with new products and services to sell to the existing markets, or explore new territories with current or new offerings? Should it improve the current technologies or try new ones? This dilemma is present not only for marketing and production strategy but in almost every investment decision.

Thus, the basic understanding of Exploration–Exploitation is as an optimization problem. And indeed, it is extensively researched as such. In probability theory, it is known as the multi-armed bandit problem. A lot of optimization strategies and computer algorithms have been developed in the last 70 years for solving that problem. The applications are wide ranging, from clinical trials and financial portfolio design, to minimizing delays in computer networks. The multi-armed bandit problem is the basis of one of the best-established areas in machine learning. Going through all these applications is beyond the objective of this chapter. It is sufficient to say that studying them is useful, as a lot of thinking, mathematics, modelling, and experimenting have been invested in with impressive results. The patterns, algorithms, and strategies which have been discovered can be useful to some extent, in certain organizational contexts. But overall, all these studies work with a lot of assumptions and simplifications which don't hold in real-life situations.

A broader understanding

The Exploration–Exploitation dilemma is present everywhere in organizations: in strategy, marketing, sales, research, operations, and projects. It appears in different guises and is communicated in various terms. Yet it is not common to hear it explicitly discussed at meetings. As James March wrote in 1991,

> *Exploration includes things captured by terms such as search, variation, risk taking, experimentation, play, flexibility, discovery, innovation. Exploitation includes such things as refinement, choice, production, efficiency, selection, implementation, execution. Adaptive systems that engage in exploration to the exclusion of exploitation are likely to find that they suffer the costs of experimentation without gaining many of its benefits. They exhibit too many undeveloped new ideas and too little distinctive competence. Conversely, systems that engage in exploitation to the exclusion of exploration are likely to find themselves trapped in suboptimal stable equilibria. As a result, maintaining an appropriate balance between exploration and exploitation is a primary factor in system survival and prosperity.*

Exploration and exploitation compete for resources, and so organizations have to make choices. Some of them are explicit, but most are implicit. The explicit choices are seen as decisions made after evaluating alternatives. A typical example is investment decisions. In comparison, implicit choices are, as March put it, "buried in many features of organizational forms and customs, for example, in organizational procedures for accumulating and reducing slack, in search rules and practices, in the ways in which targets are set and changed, and in incentive systems".

Today it is common to say that such implicit choices are part of the organizational culture. Culture is an attractive explanatory tool and a popular shoulder-shrug reflex: "It's the culture, you know." Culture is powerful. It feeds on strategies, resists change, and makes mergers heroic endeavours. It's vague and tolerant, which makes it convenient, no matter how complex the phenomena are. But precisely because it is vague and tolerant it will be avoided here, where instead we use glasses to see clearly. Simplistic explanations are not satisfactory. For example, organizational norms for tolerating slack are not just (part of the) culture. It's an implicit decision using Exploration–Exploitation balances. And it's even more than that; it is a balance itself. I call it "Requisite Inefficiency" and we'll explore it in the next chapter.

Working with the Exploration–Exploitation balance does not only help with seeing the exploitation and exploration patterns in organizational communications and decisions. It also shifts the attitude to what's really going on, away from what is accepted as rational or intuitive.

For example, a quick-learning new employee starts contributing to the organization sooner. She does so by being able to absorb the organizational knowledge quicker. That may be good for her and for the organization in the short term, but it might be bad in the long run. The organization does not have sufficient time to learn from her.

When a slow learner joins the organization, it will take longer for him to fit in, but that might actually improve the organizational knowledge and norms. Not fitting might make some shortcomings of the established ways more visible. And the same person, when well established, will be slow to absorb new knowledge. This will often be healthy conservatism, as it reduces the risk of investing in fads.

It's not just that the contribution of newcomers is different compared to what their speed of learning would have us expect;

there are more surprises. It appears also at the level of staff turnover. Seen through the lens of the Exploration–Exploitation balance, staff turnover might not look so bad. We can compare it with the evaporation rate of the ant pheromones. No turnover matches the situation with the ant colony that has everlasting pheromone trails. In other words, some level of staff turnover is healthy. It reduces the consequences of the conformity of the employees well-adapted to the company norms and beliefs.

Seeing Exploration

The results from exploitation are usually known. The potential results from exploration are always unknown. No wonder exploration is often seen as a luxury. It is practised as much as it can be afforded or when exploitation is not possible. Business cases for exploitation are much easier to defend. Exploitation practices are improved faster than exploration practices, which makes exploration more prone to fail and more difficult to justify. That's why exploration needs extra attention. For our third pair of glasses to work well, we need to first get better at recognizing exploration.

One good tip is to look for the word "search" in the name or in the definition of an activity. Searching is exploring. It's easy to see it in operations where the name contains "search", e.g. "research". And indeed, any research is exploration. In companies, there are two common kinds. They have different natures, but both are exploration. One kind is market research and the other is activities under the umbrella of Research and Development (R&D). The former concerns gathering information about markets. The latter is the activity for improving existing, and developing new, products and services. While market research is practised by companies, R&D is also common for governments.

If seeing exploration in activities labelled as "search" is easy, it's a bit more difficult when it is hidden in the organizational parlance.

One such example is recruitment. There is no "search" in the name. But what is recruitment? It is searching for new employees (or new talent, as is now the vogue). Now "search" is contained in the description, and it's easier to see recruitment as exploration.

The same with so-called sales funnels. Those on top of the funnel explore – they're sometimes called prospects. They browse a website, enter a store, or respond in some way when addressed by marketing communication. Most of them stay at the mouth of the funnel, but some show more interest and get classified as leads, prospects, and so on until a few reach the bottom of the funnel and become clients. These practices vary depending on the industry. Yet, it's common and well established that every part of the funnel should be kept full at all times. This is, in fact, the balance between exploration and exploitation encoded as a rule of thumb in marketing and sales. A company explores the market by filling the top of the funnel, and by enticing some to the bottom of the funnel, it starts to exploit it. The consumer perspective is different, yet exploration and exploitation apply equally. You browse shops (explore shops) and then you make a purchase (exploit a shop) and then potentially you use it (exploit a purchase). Back to the company perspective, filling the sales funnel can simply be defined as searching for clients, and again "search" is the key to identify it as exploration.

Organizations explore not only markets and possibilities for new products and services. They also look for ways to do things better, to do them differently, or do different things. It could be improving a process, changing the office space, implementing a new information system, or restructuring operations. In all these cases, it's about making some change in the organization. Such changes are traditionally managed as projects. Projects are regarded as a good way of organizing the work for implementing a change. That's why there is a lot of attention on improving project management worldwide. There are methodologies, books, templates, and tools. There are project management organizations with highly respected training and certification programmes. They have chapters in each country organizing lots of events.

Yet, the research organizations keep finding that the majority of projects fail. It's repeatedly reported as something bad. Well, admittedly not for everybody. It is, in fact, a very good thing for some participants in the ecosystem. Project failure statistics provide fuel for consulting practices, help promote project management courses, and drive efforts to come up with new methods. That doesn't change the statistics much, which propels more innovation.

The changed methods and practices are challenged again and again, but projects as a way of managing change are rarely questioned.

That's a pity, yet we're not going to start a discussion on the usefulness of projects as an approach for managing change, valuable as it may be. I will instead invite you to see the failure rate of projects as the exertion of the Exploration–Exploitation balance. Indeed, projects that fail can be seen as part of potential exploration. Why exploration? Because trying things out, even when big investments are involved, at a macro scale, is a way to see what works. Why potential? One reason is that not every organization is able to learn from failed projects. Another is that most failed projects continue in denial long after they have failed. There is more attention on ways to save projects than on early detection of those that will bring only cost and no value. Why is it that something that justified investment and possibly created enthusiasm can lose its value? Often, it's because the reason to do that project is not valid anymore, or because the project turned out not to be feasible. Sometimes the particular configuration of stakeholders, team, and technologies will not make a project successful, no matter what attempts are made to save it. Detection of failure, however, should not be based on a project's metrics alone. More on that in the "Productive Paradoxes" chapter.

If projects that promise organizational change are, at least to some extent, exploration, then they should be managed as such. And those with pure exploratory nature should be small and safe to fail.

However, as all projects are partly exploratory – we'll see why in the next section – their structure should allow exploration. Many organizations have realized that. Fixed-length, short iterations, ending with a prototype – especially in software projects – is a practice of disciplined exploration. A part, or nothing, of the prototype developed in one iteration is reused in the next iteration, until a more stable project product starts to take shape.

Exploration and Exploitation in space

Although the Exploration–Exploitation balance is heavily researched in game theory, optimization, and organizational studies, an essential feature has been missed. This balance works at different scales (just like Autonomy–Cohesion and Stability–Diversity). It resembles a fractal. In other words, in the context of exploitation, again there is a balance between the two, as well as in the context of exploration. And then we find it again if we zoom into the newly revealed balances. The following examples show that. We are going to zoom in to the personal level first, then zoom out to companies, then to society, and back to companies.

When viewing a painting in a museum, you consume it with your eyes. That is exploitation. But sight itself combines exploitation (perception) and exploration (eye movement). At the next level, that of your body, there is also exploration. Museum visitors explore by moving their bodies, trying out different angles and distances.

In my new strategy with jazz festivals when there aren't any known and preferred musicians, deciding to go anyway has a heavy exploration bias and would be way too risky. After all, the opportunity cost of going is not doing something else instead, which is potentially more valuable. My approach is to research some of the musicians. This splits the exploration path into exploitation (newly known and chosen) and exploration (still unknown).

It is similar with the restaurants example. If only one person chooses tested and preferred restaurants, that is pure exploitation from the perspective of that person and potentially mixed for others. If the same person chooses, but she selects somewhere not yet tested, it has elements of exploitation (the choice is confined by her knowledge and taste) and exploration (being an experiment for her as well).

In companies, some employees contribute more to exploration, others to exploitation (remember the slow and quick learners). Recruitment is both exploring and exploiting the "labour market", as the economists call it. While marketing and research are explorations from a company perspective, within these operations there are both exploration and exploitation. Many projects are explorations, but in any project there is a search for solutions (exploration) and implementation of solutions (exploitation).

This fractal nature is present also at the level of society. There we can see research and science in general as exploration. The industrial application of research we can see as exploitation. Yet both have elements of exploitation and exploration. From a macro perspective, companies exploit, but from their perspective, they also explore. They do so through their market and product research, as shown previously. Companies explore not only in research but also in operations when searching for ways to improve their core processes.

Within research (science), there is market-driven research (exploitation) and curiosity-driven research (exploration). And then market-driven research has both exploration and exploitation aspects, as does the curiosity-driven research.

The natural tendency to favour exploitation is strongly pronounced in difficult times. After the economic crisis of 2008, there was a trend in science funding to prefer and support market-driven research over curiosity-driven research. This was clear from the policies and actions of funding organizations. Exploitation typically has more constraints, better coordination, and top-down decision-making. This should already hint at a relationship with another balance. And indeed, there is such a link, but we'll come back to that point later. The concrete manifestation of the exploitation regime after the economic crisis of 2008, was observed in the selection criteria for research grants, in the framework programmes and joint programming initiatives (increased coordination), and public–private partnerships (the market directly influencing research).

Staying at a global scale, let's now look again at companies, and particularly at start-ups.

There are a large number of start-ups, but only a few are successful. Two-thirds of those that are successful have changed their initial plans. The phenomenon of start-ups and what they do, is in fact, the exploration, global and local, of new opportunities and ideas for new products and services. The successful ones are exploiting (and again exploring). At any moment, there are well-established companies, new start-ups, failed ones, and successful ones. The successful start-ups are not only exploiting. Studies have found that the majority of successful start-ups had changed their initial plans. By switching and trying out different things, they were exploring until they found a successful formula to exploit, which would turn them into viable businesses.

Each start-up tries out different strategies, while the start-ups themselves are the different trials of the market. We can see exploration and exploitation at these two levels. Yet the two levels are slightly different. What seems important at the macro level is quantity. It takes a good number of start-ups to yield a few viable businesses. And it's not only with start-ups. We also need a lot of prospects so we can turn some into clients – the sales funnel. At the lower level, we can distinguish different quality. Some ideas turn out to be good, others not. It was similar with staff turnover. Some level of turnover (quantity) is healthy. And then, at the lower level, the type of newcomers (quality) matters. We compared quick and slow learners, but that's of course just one dimension.

This was an exploration of the Exploration–Exploitation balance in space, literally and metaphorically. As we did with the other balances, it is equally important to see it in time.

Exploration and Exploitation in time

Exploitation follows exploration. We first explore the menu, select, order, and then consume what we've ordered (or what we think we've ordered). A pharmaceutical company carries out a lot of experiments to come up with a new formula which will work against a certain disease. These experiments may be futile or fruitful or, in fact, come up with something that does not treat the intended disease but turns out to be useful against another. In the first case, that exploratory path does not end in exploitation, but in the other two, it does, in an expected or an unexpected way. What's common is that exploration comes first and then exploitation.

Yet we can see the exploration and exploitation in such a sequence only if we focus on a particular element, such as choosing the food in a restaurant. But things are connected, and they interact all the time. If I go to explore a forest, I do that by exploiting my shoes. The pharmaceutical company carries out experiments exploiting laboratory equipment. Spacecraft explore the universe by exploiting various technologies.

In these examples, exploration and exploitation go in parallel, and they are coordinated, but the object of exploration and the object of exploitation is different. I'm exploring the forest, but exploiting my shoes when doing that, not the forest. The pharmaceutical company and the spacecraft also have different objects of exploration and exploitation. However, there are some cases when exploration and exploitation can have the same object and happen at the same time. And this can work pretty well.

One such case is Twitter. Sharing a tweet using the so-called "re-tweet", was neither designed nor planned as a feature in the initial releases of Twitter. People simply started tweeting others' tweets, adding "RT" for re-tweet, and this was taken up and became viral. Then both Twitter and apps and services in the Twitter ecosystem added a lot of features around RT. It evolved this way because people were exploring Twitter, and at the same time they were exploiting it. That exploration produced many other ways of using it which did not catch on, or at least not to the point of becoming one of the core capabilities of the service.

Something similar happens in the mobile apps markets. By the first quarter of 2020, there were over 2.5 million apps on the Google Play store and over 1.8 million on the Apple app store. By making it easy for the app writers to release new versions and simple for the app users to install and update, an ecosystem was created that was quite different from the traditional software world. When releasing new apps and features, app writers explore the market while at the same time exploiting it. Each app and each feature work as an almost unbiased market survey. At the same time, they are actual businesses, actual exploitation, with revenue being generated either by ads or by selling the app.

It's similar for the users. They don't know what will fit their needs and preferences. While trying out new apps and features, app users are also using them, in this way exploring and exploiting at the same time.

Depending on the perspective (user or provider) and the zoom level (features, apps, or market participants), we can see different dynamics. At the level of a single app, this period of parallel exploration and exploitation evolves into exploitation only, but if we zoom out, we'll see that they keep running in parallel. While being used to certain apps, users keep exploiting the app market. By utilizing new apps (a level up) or new features (a level down), they co-explore with the app writers.

App writers, both individual and companies, compete by improving the existing capabilities and releasing new ones. Some of them develop new apps, entering again into a mode of parallel compressed exploration and exploitation. The balance can be seen at the next level as well, the level of the developers (entrepreneurs). New ones come and some grow, others go. The invisible hand of the market produces entrepreneurs who try out new things and stay (exploit) if they are successful and leave if not.

Going to jazz festivals taught me a lesson about the balance between exploration and exploitation. Observing app markets shows what it is to explore *while* exploiting. But for an example of the latter, I could've just stayed at the jazz festival. Jazz improvisation is where exploitation and exploration run in parallel to form a compressed and precarious balance. With classical music, exploration and exploitation are separated in time and space. A composer explores by trying out different harmonies and melodies, and later on, an orchestra exploits the composed fixed sequence of chords and notes with a prescribed length and manner of playing. In a jazz band, composing and performing happen at the same time. Each musician is exploring and exploiting the territory marked by the main theme, their own ideas and others' inventions and provocations. It takes a long time and hard work to reach that level of awareness, intuition, and skill. Musicians put in many years of practice to produce just a few minutes of good unprepared music. The years of preparation supply jazz musicians with both an arsenal of patterns to use when short of ideas (exploit), and the skills necessary to break out of them (explore).

Twitter, the app market, and jazz improvisation show the

benefits of compressed or simultaneous exploration/exploitation. That doesn't mean it's always good when the balance is achieved this way. To suggest so is to give a prescription. And you could easily come up with a daily example challenging such a suggestion. When you search for a good wine and there is no tasting option, you have to buy and try bottle after bottle until you find one that you like. As with the idea for the exploratory projects that should be safe to fail in the mode of simultaneous exploration and exploitation, the size of the investment is important. A bottle is too big a chunk (and price to pay) for such an exploration. In other cases, there are other important factors besides size. Overall, sequential and simultaneous exploration/exploitation are applicable in different circumstances, and maybe, in the long run, should also be balanced.

There seems to be, however, a correlation between the size of the cycle of each mode, and the level of uncertainty in the environment.

For organizations, over-exploiting will either exhaust the external resources they are exploiting or make them slow to adapt, less competitive, and eventually they are driven out of the market. In contrast, over-exploring exhausts organizations' own resources. To maintain the balance is always necessary for survival. However, depending on the level of complexity and uncertainty, it might not be sufficient just to maintain it, but how the balance is kept becomes crucial.

In biological evolution, sight might be considered as one of the most impressive achievements. For species that excel in seeing, such as an eagle, perception (exploitation) happens together and is complemented by eye movement (exploration). The evolutionary advantage of not just balancing, but bringing exploration and exploitation closer together, applies to organizations as well, as the examples of Twitter and app markets show. While an eagle has some idea of what it will perceive (exploit) and discover (explore) as it soars above its territory, the app market has much more uncertainty, as the various players sell (exploit) and innovate (explore) all at the same time, creating and reshaping their territory by their actions.

The more uncertain the environment, the more that exploration and exploitation following each other in shorter cycles may be beneficial, and the more organizations need to invent new business models where exploration and exploitation go together or are both characteristics of one and the same activity.

Enabling Exploration

When Exploration–Exploitation is out of balance, it's often towards exploitation. Organizations usually over-exploit and under-explore. That's why "Seeing Exploration" was devoted to recognizing exploration in various organizational activities. In a way, this was extended when we looked at the balance in space, where exploration was discovered inside exploitation and vice versa. Exploration can appear in different search-related activities, or it can be found in any exploitation one level up or down. Once there is a habit of revealing exploration, it should also be easier to see when an organization, or a part of it, is under-exploring. But what can we do to achieve or restore the balance?

You might expect the answer to this question would be some kind of tip or advice, or even a pointer to best practices for maintaining the balance. As I explained at the beginning of the book, I'll refrain from giving recipes and prescriptions. What I offer instead is a better way of seeing certain structural relationships that seem to be invariant for organizations. When it comes to exploration and exploitation, the focus is the relation with constraints. To exploit, constraints need to be added, while to explore, constraints need to be released. Exploitation can be managed, but exploration can only be enabled.

Enabling is achieved by reducing and releasing constraints. That could mean doing something more, doing something less, or doing something differently. We need to do something more when we can help reduce constraints to enable exploration. We need to do something less when we have imposed constraints. And we need to do something differently when the current way of doing it is constraining exploration.

Imagine a child in your house (son, nephew, grandson), who wants to make dinner for you. He needs to find a good recipe, but he doesn't know where to look for it. You can help by giving him the available cookbooks in the house. That effort will enable exploration, but only to some extent. The exploration range will still be limited to the set of recipes contained in those books. The means for searching will also be limited to the table of contents and the book index. If you give the child an electronic device with a browser connected to the internet, this will expand his exploration possibilities. In case he is constrained by a limited knowledge of how to use the device (not likely these days), then teaching him how to use it would further enable him, as would some tips on where to look for good recipes. These four activities, giving cookbooks, providing a device with a browser, teaching him to use it, and advising on websites with good recipes, are all examples of lifting constraints by doing more to enable exploration. Yet the last two enter a tricky zone. Certain teaching approaches can restrict the child to the way you use the device, thus limiting exploration of novel ways. And then depending on how you present the recommended websites, this might prevent him from exploring outside them.

Ants explore without constraints. When they find a food source, they take a piece and bring it back to the nest, leaving a pheromone trail. That's a way to communicate with other ants and guide them. The pheromone trail is the constraint. Ants stop exploring and start exploiting. Initially, some ants follow it, reinforce it, and then more ants follow. When there is less food left, fewer ants refresh the trail and it evaporates. The constraint disappears, enabling new exploration.

Remember the story of Ferenc from the first chapter? He complained that in most assignments it's determined not only what to do, but also how, when the missing know-how was the reason to hire him in the first place. That's a typical example where exploration can be enabled by doing less, by explaining why and defining what, but not how. Defining how is a constraint that limits exploration. That is especially relevant for knowledge-intensive tasks and for any kind of assignment that has an element of innovation. But should there be any assignment without implicit or explicit invitation to innovate?

And lastly, we can enable exploration by doing things differently. Especially when innovating. There is a circularity here. Innovation is finding ways to do things differently. But to enable it, we already need to do things differently so that some constraints are relaxed.

When running process improvement workshops, for example, I noticed that people were way too limited by self-imposed constraints when generating ideas. Self-imposed constraints are not bad per se. They can be helpful when creating something. So-called "writer's block" is partly caused by the infinite possibilities offered by the blank page. Adding some constraints can be helpful. Yet, when exploring ideas for improvement, self-imposed constraints can limit innovation. In my process improvement workshops, they were held dear as people felt good about giving only realistic proposals. And indeed, most of the constraints were real. They were legal and administrative limitations, capacity constraints, and norms. Yet, when those constraints were made explicit, deconstructed, and lifted for a while, we got better results. We kept some of the unconstrained ideas, or others provoked by them. When the constraints were put back, these ideas either turned out to be feasible or triggered insights on how to deal with the constraints. (We'll look at this example from another perspective in the "Productive Paradoxes" chapter.)

But there are constraints that are much more difficult to lift. Some of them are so deeply embedded in our language and thinking, that it requires a lot of effort and practice to get them out of the way and bring them back at will. One such thing is the way we think about time.

Earlier, when we looked at exploration and exploitation in time, we saw that they can come in sequence, they can happen in parallel, or they can be two characteristics of the same activity. But what about the way we perceive and talk about time? It seems that we don't have a concept of time in and of itself. We cannot think about time in terms of time, but only in terms of events, space, and motion.

Events are something that help distinguish between before and after. They cannot unhappen, and that's why time is irreversible. By counting event and cycles, we are able to measure time.

Events and cycles are not sufficient. To achieve the rich understanding of time that we have, we use other concepts, such as space and motion. Understanding time in terms of space and motion is deeply rooted in language. We leave something behind, and our future is in front of us. We can only be at a certain location, because we came from where we were earlier and that is now behind us. Next, we are going to a destination that is an extension of the line that connects our past with our present. Useful as it may be, this notion constrains our thinking and lifting that constraint can be beneficial for exploration and dealing with uncertainty.

A good proposal for that comes from the Quantum Approach to Time and Organizational Change (QATC). It is a different way of thinking about time, based on quantum mechanics and quantum probability theories. QATC sees the future as qualitatively different from the present and the past. It can be perceived as their continuation only in retrospect. The authors suggest that we mentally reverse the arrow of time and see the future as having many potentialities:

> *Because many future potentialities may exist in an indefinite state until they are conjoined with a context, they cannot be known until they are tried out. Thus, exploration is a fundamental part of creating entirely new and different futures.*
>
> — LORD ET AL.

Instead of thinking that time flows from past to present to future, QATC suggests imagining time flowing from future to present. Each particular state, or the present, is selected, or rather, enacted, by the specific configuration of organizational unit, context, and technology. Most of the potentialities are not directly experienced and through retrospection can be seen as something that might have happened. QATC proposes using counterfactual thinking to examine what could have been different. Counterfactual thinking can help "to understand how a present is selected from many different potential alternatives that once existed in the future, rather than how the past leads to one future state". The particular interaction of constraints and processes in an organization makes certain potentialities develop more than others. Those that develop more, form attractors that channel processes in definite and consistent ways.

For exploration to work, there is one more constraint to be relaxed. And that's the fear of mistakes. In a culture where mistakes are punished, people avoid taking risks. In it is only by trying, by taking risks, and by inevitably making many errors, that we can explore and learn.

To summarize, exploration needs to be enabled. Enabling means lifting constraints. That could be done by doing something more, for example, providing exploration devices and knowledge. It could be done by doing something less, such as limiting to *why* and *what* when giving assignments, instead of also specifying *how*. And last, it can be done by doing something differently, for example, temporarily lifting constraints when generating improvement ideas, reversing the arrow of time when thinking about the future, and accepting errors as a natural and useful in every exploration.

Looking at yourself looking at something

The three balances are closely related. We explore when lifting constraints, but we impose constraints to exploit. The relationship between Exploration–Exploitation and Autonomy–Cohesion is then quite direct. Enabling autonomy is enabling exploration, while exploitation requires more rules, coordination, planning, and in general, more coherence. More coherence – you probably remember – is achieved by more constraints.

And then exploitation requires stability, while exploration benefits from diversity. Understanding each balance in its own right has benefits, and so does complementing the knowledge and habits of thinking in terms of one balance with those of another balance. But there is also a way to use one balance on top of another.

Imagine you have been wearing the Stability–Diversity glasses for quite some time and you are finding them extremely useful, as you would. The more useful they are and the more benefits they give you for diagnosing and improving, the more likely you are to use them often. The associated thinking habits will also become stronger.

Now imagine you film yourself wearing your Stability–Diversity glasses. What you'll probably see is that you are successfully using the Stability–Diversity glasses and because of that you keep wearing them. But if you watch yourself doing that with Exploration–Exploitation glasses on, you'll immediately realize what's going on.

You are wearing the Stability–Diversity glasses for too long.

You are over-exploiting. So, you should stop, you should take them off or try on other glasses.

You can find yourself over-exploiting your Stability–Diversity glasses or your Autonomy–Cohesion glasses. Wearing Exploration–Exploitation glasses for too long is also over-exploiting. And it applies not only to the balances of this book. It applies to any idea or theory that you like. This is important and deserves more attention.

An idea might appear attractive at first glance, or after years of digging and testing, or both. When it looks instantly convincing, it just resonates with your experience. There are so many things that such an idea can help you see in a new light, or help you fill some old explanatory gaps. Or, it can sound absurd when you first hear it, and then later it gets under your skin. Either way, you buy into it.

There are four problems with such attachment. One is that, like purchasing a car or a house, it has a maintenance cost. You might find yourself protecting it only because you invested in it. The other three problems you see through the glasses: you have less autonomy, you are experiencing less diversity, and you are over-exploiting and under-exploring. And that's the main reason I keep using the glasses metaphor. It's a reminder that glasses have frames; they create bias and leave a blind spot. They should fit well, they are yours, but they are not you. You can take them off at will.

Let's return to the situation when you find yourself over-exploiting your Stability–Diversity glasses. What do you see if you take them off? Well, there are other useful ways to look at organizations for which even the richness of the three balances contained in Stability–Diversity glasses can be limiting.

Thinking in terms of stability, for example, is prone to stabilize the understanding of organizational change as something episodic. That is well supported by the tradition in the sciences to study movement as a sequence of state transitions. Ironically, the mathematical description of movement is made through concepts lacking movement. Change itself is used in organizations more often as a noun and not as a verb. But organizations are constantly changing at every level. Not only to maintain stability, not only to improve, they simply can't stop changing as long as they exist.

> *Change must not be thought of as a property of organization. Rather, organization must be understood as an emergent property of change.*
>
> — Thoukas and Chia

There are other benefits of the mental exercise where you use a pair of glasses to look at yourself looking at a situation with another pair of glasses. Imagine that you are again wearing the Stability–Diversity glasses. And then one day you find evidence for the benefits of homogeneity, for example, for building trust. We have already taken care with the risks of too much diversity. Now, through an Exploration–Exploitation lens, we can see more and extend our understanding. For better exploration, the Diversity balance should favour heterogeneity. However, it needs to shift towards homogeneity for better exploitation.

Last, let's look at Exploration–Exploitation with Autonomy–Cohesion glasses on. How should that balance be maintained? Should we give autonomy to the organizational units to decide? It might be too risky to completely release control over such an important thing. Maybe it should be regulated and embedded in the organizational structure and rules. Or rather, we need to be alert and consciously balance autonomy and cohesion to enable the balance between exploration and exploitation.

Summary

Organizations at all levels are exploring and exploiting. From ant colonies to human society, they need to balance these activities to survive and be successful.

We balance exploration and exploitation daily and throughout our life. That balance determines both short- and long-term experience. Enjoying food, viewing art, and listening to music are dependent on it. Not only the immediate, but also the long-term experience, is better when based on decisions balancing exploitation and exploration. Experimenting with restaurants, museums, and concerts will always – at the price of a higher risk of disappointment – increase the opportunities for valuable discoveries.

What applies to leisure decisions also applies to life decisions, but with graver consequences. If we decide to invest our time in improving what we currently do well, we'll get even better. But the price is not allocating time to trying out new things. This may put us in a difficult situation when there is no more demand for what we are skilled at.

Balancing exploration and exploitation is, at first glance, a resource allocation decision. Should you exploit a resource, refine a technology, and extend the offering to existing clients? Or should you look for alternative resources, new technologies, and explore new markets? It is equally a viability decision. An animal needs to eat (exploit) to have the energy to look for more food (explore). A company needs a flow of resources now, so that it can finance research and innovation to ensure its viability in the future.

Some of these choices are obvious. For example, in investment decisions. Others are hidden in organizational structures, rules, and norms.

Organizations tend to over-exploit and under-explore. This is natural. The expected results from exploitation are usually known, while the potential results from exploration are always unknown. There is certainty and immediate return from exploitation. Exploration is prone to fail and difficult to defend. That's why we need to pay more attention to it. First, to be able to recognize it and then to enable it.

For recognizing, it's helpful to notice whether an activity contains "search" in its name or definition (respectively "use" for exploitation).

For enabling, we should reduce or release constraints. That could mean doing something more, doing something less, or doing something differently. We need to do something more when we can help by reducing constraints to enable exploration. We need to do something less when we have imposed constraints. And we need to do something differently when the current way of doing it is constraining exploration.

To hone the new skill, as we did with previous balances, we explored the Exploration–Exploitation balance in space and time.

In space, exploration and exploitation work at different scales. There is exploration and exploitation within each exploitation and exploration. Another dimension in space is along whole/part and who/what perspectives, which are easy to observe in the mobile apps ecosystem: features, apps, developers, and market.

In time, the usual sequence is exploration and then exploitation, but sometimes they can either follow each other in very short cycles or be two characteristics of the same activity. With the current hyper-connectivity and pace of change, there might be an increase in sighting organizations and ecosystems in compressed Exploration–Exploitation mode.

The three essential balances are related. Exploration requires more autonomy and diversity. Exploitation can be achieved when there is coherence and stability. But we can learn even more if we use the lens of one balance to look at another. We may even challenge the balance itself, such as when looking at a situation with the same pair of glasses for too long.

Autonomy–Cohesion, Stability–Diversity, and Exploration–Exploitation are the three essential balances in organization. Since we have described them, this book could end here. But along the way we have seen how these balances are related. How autonomy somehow goes along with diversity and exploration. And how cohesion is in some way related to stability and exploitation. Could there be a balance encompassing all three? Some sort of a meta-balance?

Yes. It turns out there is another pair of glasses that is extremely useful. It's a bit more abstract. It's a bit more difficult to make it a habit. But it's well worth the effort because its applications are very powerful.

NOTES

1. "I restrict the world to what I can imagine or permit…"

The quote and the following story are from "Try again. Fail again. Fail better: The cybernetics in design and the design in cybernetics" (Glanville, 2007).

2. [I]n each colony it takes a different time for a pheromone trail to evaporate.

The characteristics of the pheromone trails are not the only factor influencing the balance between exploration and exploitation and respectively the foraging efficiency. Other factors such as group foraging and whether the colony inhabits one or several socially connected nests contribute as well (Cook, Franks, & Robinson, 2013).

3. In probability theory, it is known as the multi-armed bandit problem.

The name "multi-armed bandit problem" comes from the one-armed bandit slot machine. If instead of a single machine, there is a row of slot machines, a gambler needs to decide which machine to play, how many times to play each machine and in what order. The dilemma in its simplest form is most clearly visible when the gambler is lucky with the current machine and needs to decide whether to continue with it or try a different one (Weber, 1992).

4. The applications are wide ranging, from clinical trials and financial portfolio design, to minimizing delays in computer networks. The multi-armed bandit problem is the basis of one of the best-established areas in machine learning.

Multi-armed bandit strategies have been used in clinical trials. Researchers are looking for ways to simultaneously identify the best treatment and ensure that as many patients as possible can benefit from it (Kuleshov & Precup, 2014) or for addressing ethical issues (Press, 2009).

Multi-armed bandit optimization techniques have also been applied in financial portfolio optimization (Shen, Wang, Jiang, & Zha, 2015) and in dynamic routing to minimize delays in computer networks (Henri, Vlachou, & Thiran, 2018).

Reinforcement learning is one of the three main types of machine learning, the other two being supervised and unsupervised learning. It is based on balancing exploitation and exploration and is particularly suited for problems that include a long-term versus short-term reward trade-off.

5. As James March wrote in 1991.

The quote is from "Exploration and Exploitation in Organizational Learning" (March, 1991).

6. Culture is powerful. It feeds on strategies, resists change, and makes mergers heroic endeavours.

"Culture eats strategy for breakfast" is a popular quote misattributed to Peter Drucker. Since it appeared circa 2000, it's been echoed endlessly, as if nothing was truer. Well, I think it is wrong.

Strategy is a pattern of behaviour. What a strategy was can be seen retrospectively. So if the Culture asks, "What's for breakfast today?", its butler should logically answer, "We'll only know tomorrow."

Some may say that the quote is about strategic plans. Well, that makes a bit more sense. And yet, planning is a matter of culture.

So, by hearing the butler's answer, the Culture might – to maintain dignity – say, "Anyway, I'm on a diet. It's tactics for me today."

7. Detection of failure, however, should not be based on a project's metrics alone.

A classic example is the Sydney Opera House project. In 1957, it was initially estimated to cost 7 million Australian dollars. It was completed in 1973 for 102 million Australian dollars (equivalent to about a billion in 2020) ten years later than estimated (New South Wales Government State Archives & Records, 2020). Using only the project metrics, it would have been justified to stop the project and minimize the loss. After all, the budget overrun was not 100% or

200%. It was over 14 times more. Yet, the new opera house revenue compensated for the budget overrun in the first years of operation.

8. But sight itself combines exploitation (perception) and exploration (eye movement).

Perception was believed (and still is by some schools in Cognitive Science) to rely on an inner representation of the outside world. That conviction was first challenged by Yarbus in the sixties (Yarbus, 1967). Then in the nineties, J. Kevin O'Regan and Alva Noë demonstrated how sensory stimulations depend on the activities of the perceiver (O'Regan & Noë, 2001). They developed the so-called sensory-motor contingency theory. Recently this notion was complemented and extended by other findings and theories. What they have in common is that, when it comes to seeing, eye movement contributes a lot to what we see. Experiments by Laeng and Teodorescu showed, for example, that exploring images is essential for the accuracy of image recall (Laeng & Teodorescu, 2002). See also Livingstone (2008).

9. Museum visitors explore by moving their bodies, trying out different angles and distances.

Art experience, just like any other human experience, is embodied. It's not the workings of a particular receptor and a zone in the brain. The whole structure of the body and its interaction with the environment determines what is and how it is experienced. There is a growing body of transdisciplinary research devoted to this. Particularly for the study of museum visitors and the choreography of their movement see Diamantopoulou and Christidou (2019).

10. There are a large number of start-ups, but only a few are successful.

Statistics on start-up failures vary greatly. Some sources claim that 90% of all start-ups fail. According to an often-cited study from Bloomberg from 2002 (Klein, 2002), the failure rate is 80%. From the more reliable sources, that might be considered the highest rate reported. At the other end of the spectrum is a recent collection of statistics from various sources made by Small Business Trends (Mansfield, 2019). According to that report, 44% of small businesses started in 2014 don't make to their fifth year. However, the same source found that only 40% of small businesses are profitable.

11. Two-thirds of those that are successful have changed their initial plans.

This is the finding of John Mullins and Randy Komisar (Mullins & Komisar, 2009).

12. By the first quarter of 2020, there were over 2.5 million apps on the Google Play store and over 1.8 million on the Apple app store.

The source of these numbers is "Number of apps available in leading app stores as of 1st quarter 2020" (2020).

13. Jazz improvisation is where exploitation and exploration run in parallel to form a compressed and precarious balance.

Frank Barrett found many similarities between jazz improvisation and what managers need to do in the contemporary dynamic and uncertain environment.

> *To be innovative, managers – like jazz musicians – must interpret vague cues, face unstructured tasks, process incomplete knowledge, and yet they must take action anyway.* (Barrett, 1998)

Jazz musicians exploit the allowances of the theme, constrained by the key signature, while at the same time exploring the territory marked by the main theme, often expanding its boundaries. During soloing, they try out novel ideas (explore), but when nothing comes to mind, the musicians cannot stop, so they exploit their bag of "licks and crips".

14. Exploitation can be managed, but exploration can only be enabled.

More precisely, exploration needs to first be enabled by lifting certain constraints. Then it can also be managed to some extent.

15. We cannot think about time in terms of time, but only in terms of events, space, and motion.

Time perception is analyzed by George Lakoff and Mark Johnson in *Philosophy In The Flesh* (Lakoff & Johnson, 2008) and in *Metaphors We Live By* (Lakoff & Johnson, 2003).

16. We leave something behind, and our future is in front of us.

There are exceptions. In the Aymara language, spoken in the Andean highlands of Bolivia, Peru, and northern Chile, the special mapping of time is the opposite of the majority of the studied languages. In Aymara, the past is in front and the future is behind (Núñez & Sweetser, 2005).

17. A good proposal for that comes from the Quantum Approach to Time and Organizational Change (QATC).

QATC (Lord, Dihn, & Hoffman, 2015) has three main advantages. By emphasizing that the future is often qualitatively different from the present or past, and using multiple interacting paths, it can represent complexity better than the conventional models. Second, using approaches from quantum physics, it can incorporate the dependency on the context and in a rigorous way. Third, it challenges fundamental assumptions about time, such as that it flows from the past through the present to the future and that phenomena of interest exist independently of our attempts to measure them.

18. [B]y taking risks, and by inevitably making many errors, that we can explore and learn.

As Kathryn Schulz wrote in *Being Wrong*, "To err is to wander, and wandering is the way we discover the world" (Schulz, 2011).

19. Thinking in terms of stability, for example, is prone to stabilize the understanding of organizational change as something episodic.

For a detailed exploration of the topic of organizational change from a perspective of change and not of stability, see Tsoukas and Chia (2002).

20. And then one day you find evidence for the benefits of homogeneity.

For an example of such evidence see Roy and Dugal (1998). Although the study is based on a very limited sample and as such is not representative, it confirms the findings of previous studies that homogeneous groups perform better. There are three clarifications that need to be made. First, the authors point out that heterogeneity should be encouraged, but managers "need to consider the cognitive flexibility of group members" (ibid.). Second, the importance of heterogeneity of agents – as demonstrated by the adaptive immune system – is higher in situations of uncertainty, and such situations were not included in the study. And the third is a confirmation of the point made in the chapter: homogeneity supports exploitation, while heterogeneity supports exploration.

21. Or rather, we need to be alert and consciously balance autonomy and cohesion to enable the balance between exploration and exploitation.

The Exploration–Exploitation balance in organizations is often referred to as "organizational ambidexterity" (O'Reilly III & Tushman, 2013). The most studied modes of organizational ambidexterity are sequential and simultaneous. Gibson and Birkinshaw, however, came up with a third type – contextual ambidexterity (Gibson & Birkinshaw, 2004). They define it as one in which there is a "supportive organizational context" that "encourages individuals to make their own judgments as to how to best divide their time between the conflicting demands".

4

STIMULI AND RESPONSES

If the rate of change on the outside exceeds the rate of change on the inside, the end is near.

— Jack Welch

Somebody throws a melon at you and you have to catch it. You do. Then she tosses a second melon your way. You happen to have excellent melon-catching skills, and you succeed in holding on to it. You now have a melon in each hand. She pitches a third melon. Remember, you are not allowed to let a melon fall on the ground. Can you keep hold of what you have and grab the incoming fruit? Oops! You drop the second one while trying to grasp the third. With four or more lobbed your way, there will be an ever-growing sticky pile of broken melons at your feet, since you won't be able to catch all of them.

As far as catching melons goes, you can cope as long as their number matches the number of your catching devices: your hands. And that's the essence of the Stimuli–Responses balance. To succeed, your responses should match the stimuli.

Said simply like this, it raises many questions. What does it mean to succeed? To succeed at what? What do stimuli refer to? All of them, or only those that matter? How to count them? What do responses refer to? Is it the number of hands? Or the number of some devices or elements? And if elements, again, how to count them? Should we count them at all?

These are all valid questions, and the chances are you have more. To answer them, we need to clarify what this balance is and how it works. As I mentioned at the end of the previous chapter, it is special. This balance can be used as a pair of glasses for all situations where we used the glasses of the other balances. Then it is revealing and potentially useful to look at them again, but with the new device. Before doing so, we need some elaboration of the balance and more examples. The one where we are pelted with fruit may be somewhat limited, yet we haven't used its full potential. Let's do that now.

Melons, lemons, and cherries

There are over 25 varieties of melons. To be able to catch the one or two thrown at you, they shouldn't be much bigger than your palm. Only a few sorts guarantee that. If you can't influence the choice of melons and you only want to catch them, then you don't need to know what sort of melons they are. All you care about is that their size isn't larger than that of your palm, and the number of melons thrown at you isn't bigger than two. But if you are allowed to specify all melons permitted for this game, you should know something about the existing melon varieties. You need to match that variety by knowing how big each kind of melon is.

Here *variety* is used as a common way to refer to different types. There is a broader way to use *variety* which has proved to be very useful. It was first proposed by Ross Ashby more than 60 years ago. He came up with a law that he called the Law of Requisite Variety.

It says that "variety destroys variety". Stafford Beer rephrased that as "only variety can absorb variety". But what is variety in this context?

One way to understand variety is as the number of different elements. The word *cuckoo* has six letters, but only four of them are different. Thus it has a variety of four. If we rewrite it with a capital C and let the difference between uppercase and lowercase letters contribute to variety, then *Cuckoo* has a variety of five. Variety is a relative measure. It depends on who is asking and why. In fact, it cannot be fully understood outside the context of the law.

Then let's repeat the law again: only variety absorbs variety. Variety is used there twice. The first refers to the variety of the one who wants to achieve something. The variety of the potential response. The second is the variety of the stimuli. You want to catch melons with your hands. If no more than two melons are thrown, you can catch them. You can only succeed if the variety of the stimuli matches the variety of the response. Two melons against two hands. So far, you can count your variety by counting your hands.

But now you have a new fruity threat looming. This time your assailant comes at you hurling lemons. One by one. You must not allow a lemon to fall on the ground. Let's assume that you are as adept at catching lemons as you were with melons. You might be able to catch and hold four, or even six lemons, three in each hand. In this case, you succeed as long as the lemon-holding capacity of your hands matches the number of lemons thrown at you. If we applied the law, your capacity alone determines your variety.

While we catch our breath before another inevitable fruit attack, let's measure the variety of words again. The variety of *cuckoo* was four. If your goal is to count the variety of a word, as long as you can distinguish these letters, you have enough variety to achieve this goal. But what about the variety of *melon* and *lemon*? It's five for both of them. If these are two hands of five playing cards, they are exactly equal in strength. But that doesn't mean there won't be a winner. The cards will be played in a certain order. And it is also (and only!) the order of the letters that helps us distinguish *melon* and *lemon*. We see now that the different type of letters, size, and order, may all participate in measuring the variety of a word. If the font or the colour of letters is different, there might be other criteria for distinction, depending on whether it matters for your goal. And then, we assumed that the elements of a word are the letters, which is a common and fair assumption. But if our goal is to print them clearly, then we are more interested in the number of pixels.

Heads up! Incoming cherry assault. This time, once you have both your hands full of cherries, you can start catching them with your mouth. Remember, the goal is to keep the cherries off the ground. Then your variety will be equal to the sum of the cherry-holding capacities of your hands and mouth. And not only that. If you happen to be wearing a skirt or a dress, you could stop a lot of cherries using the upper part of your body and then trap them in your lap.

For the nature of this game, what matters most is the size of the fruit. But no less important are your reflexes and agility. So, a lot of things can contribute to variety: reaction time, speed, and precision of movement, capacity, what clothes you are wearing, your decision about which hand to use when, and so on.

All these factors contributing to variety are not absolute. They depend on what you want to achieve. If your goal is to catch only one piece of fruit, then you may succeed regardless of the size of the melon. For lemons and cherries, you may also do something else in parallel. The variety of the responses that matters for the balance depends on your goal. Same for the variety of stimuli. Some of it might be safe to ignore. The variety of stimuli that you can potentially register will also depend on the limits of your perception.

All that might sound like stating the obvious. What is not so obvious is how widespread this balance is.

It's everywhere

Look around you. What do the things you see have in common? Most of them sit and stand on the ground or on top of each other, because of what we call gravity. And yes, some float in the air or on the water. But even then they can't escape gravity.

Like gravity, the balance between stimuli and responses is omnipresent. Whenever there is purpose and interaction, it's there. It was in every story so far. Remember, for example, the story of Ferenc from the first chapter? Every situation there can be seen as a balance between stimuli and responses. But we are not going to go through that now. Instead, let's see what happened on that same morning, but this time with Emma.

Emma's Morning

Emma woke, glanced at her clock, and saw that it was a bit after six. Then she realized it was only half-past midnight. She had misread the clock, which had hands almost the same size. Luckily, she was soon sleeping again.

When it was actually six, she was already about to make herself a coffee. She had woken up some minutes earlier with a stiff neck. Now, waiting for the coffee machine to warm up, Emma tried stretching her neck by gently pulling her head and shoulder in opposite directions.

She was thinking about the mail she had to write to Ferenc. She had forgotten to invite him for the meeting at two and now she also needed to tell him that the evaluation report had a new, probably impossible, deadline. She was frowning at the thought when the indicator showed the coffee machine was ready. Emma pressed the button. She pulled her smartphone from the pocket of her nightgown to check the weather. The screen was dirty. The machine announced with a beep that the coffee was ready. She took out the cup, then tried to wipe her phone screen with a dry napkin. That didn't work. She successfully cleaned it with a slightly wet tissue. She forgot what she needed the phone for and started checking her agenda. After a few sips of coffee, she went to take a shower.

What she had seen on her agenda wasn't pleasant. More things were due that week than she had thought. While thinking about that, she was failing to get the shower to the right temperature. The water was either too hot or too cold.

The temperature outside was going to vary as well. This was what she found out when she finally checked the forecast some minutes later. She had an initial idea for what to wear today, which she was going to ditch for a layered alternative. But then she remembered that she was mostly going to be in the office the whole day, and when she wasn't, she would be in her car. So, she decided to stay with her original clothing plan.

Half an hour later, Emma was driving to the office. She missed the green light at the first big intersection by a second and had to stop. There were no cars passing in front on the crossing street, while behind her the queue was growing. It was stupid, she thought. Intersections like that shouldn't be controlled with traffic lights. A roundabout would have been much more suitable. The throughput would be based on the traffic, not on the mindless cycle of the traffic lights.

She had read about the Magic Roundabout in Swindon, UK. It is in fact, five mini-circles around a sixth bigger one. This creates a configuration of seven roundabouts: an outer circle and the five mini-roundabouts going clockwise, and the inner circle going anticlockwise. It sounds like a nightmare and many drivers think it is. Yet, it's been there since 1972 and statistics show it's both faster and safer to go through compared to other similar junctions.

She got a green light and pressed the accelerator, her thoughts moving to a project for which she badly needed a green light as well. On the highway, she drove for less than five minutes before she was halted by congestion. Surrounded by cars, she considered what kind of arguments she could bring and what kind of support she could get for the project. Her thoughts were interrupted by occasional honking. Honking reminded her of baby cries. Babies want to communicate various emotions, but when they try, it comes out as one and the same cry. *Well, not to their mums, I guess,* Emma thought.

The traffic on the other side of the highway was light. She saw an exotic vintage car approaching. As it passed, she watched it to the point allowed by her neck, which was still stiff and painful.

Emma arrived at her desk just after eight-thirty. She answered a couple of emails. Then she wrote that mail to Ferenc and right after forwarded him the invitation for the meeting in the afternoon. Then it was time to leave for her first meeting.

There were five people in the meeting. They had all arrived earlier and were already discussing the situation with the new competitor, which is what the meeting was about. During the 90 minutes of the meeting, several options from different perspectives were discussed. In the end, it seemed there were two ways to deal with it: either increase their product range to match the competitor's best-selling lines, or merge with the competitor. The latter was appealing. It had the additional advantage of eliminating one competitor. But it posed other issues.

Were you able to spot how many times the balance appeared in this story? The answer is ten. Let's go through them one by one.

First is the misreading of the clock. We want a clock to show us the time. For everyday use, if we can distinguish minutes, that's good enough. An analogue clock shows 12 hours. That makes 720 minutes. Then the variety of an analogue clock is 720. We tell the time by the position of the two hands. They should have 720 positions that we can distinguish. But there are some fancy analogue clocks that compromise that to look nice or original. And it seems this was the case with Emma's clock. When the clock hands are of similar size, then they don't clearly communicate the variety of the clock mechanism. Two different times, such as 12:30 and 6:03, can look almost the same.

The dry napkin wasn't much use when Emma tried to use it to clean her smartphone screen. It didn't have requisite variety. The wet tissue, as expected, did. Physics comes with a theory of cohesive and adhesive forces, surface tension, and suchlike to explain why this is the case. It is a useful theory. But unlike the balance between stimuli and responses (and the Law of Requisite Variety that it's based on), it can't be applied to other situations. The wet tissue brought the needed variety that the dry napkin was lacking. This made the variety of the response (cleaning) sufficient to match or exceed the variety of the stimuli, the dirt on the phone screen.

The sensation of the water from a shower tells us if we should turn the handle to the blue or to the red to get the desired temperature. We might not have the potential variety to achieve that. If the heating is not working, then no matter what we do, we can't get the desired water sensation. But sometimes, even when it is technically achievable, it's our responses that might not have the requisite variety. This was the case with Emma. She saw that she had more things due for the week than expected. This made her anxious and impatient. When impatient, we tend to overreact. That wasn't good when she tried to use her mixer faucet to get the water temperature right. When we make a change, it always takes time for the faucet to produce a response. So, when Emma didn't get the desired effect in a reasonable time, she turned the handle more in the same direction. With the water still not hot enough, she again turned the handle to the red. It was still cold, and she turned it yet further. Then, because of the delay, the water suddenly came out way too hot. In trying not to get scalded, she reacted the opposite way and overshot her goal in the other direction, shocked by a freezing cold jet. We need to learn the nature of the delay between our reaction and its effect to bring sufficient variety of our responses.

The next example again concerns temperature regulation.

Both Ferenc and Emma checked the forecast and saw that the temperature was going to vary greatly during the day. They both initially decided to respond to this variety by increasing the number of layers of clothing. But Emma did not go for it because she could afford a different response due to her more protective means of transport. It's a natural thing to keep ourselves in the comfort zone. Most of us don't see that as a balance between stimuli and responses. We don't think that by adding layers or buffers we increase our variety. But the law exerts itself anyway. Likewise, hawks don't think they use gravity to catch their prey.

Traffic lights are a clear and rich example of how the balance works. The simplest traffic light device just follows a cycle. It needs four states to communicate stop, go, attention, and not working. Then traffic lights are good enough if they can have a variety of four. But in fact, if each light is on and off and we ignore the flashing state, then we have a variety of eight (two to the power of three equals eight). Adding the flashing state for each light, the variety of a standard traffic light reaches 27. In both cases, it's more than the needed variety, which is four for stop, go, attention, and not working. And anyway, for practical reasons, most of the possible combinations don't give clear and simple signals.

There are traffic control systems called "adaptive" for they can adapt to the traffic. In other words, they consider the variety of the traffic and in doing so, increase the variety of their response. Yet, the drivers do not take part in that control.

Roundabouts are different. There is no device used there. The situation created physically by the construction, together with the traffic rules, uses the distributed cognition of the drivers to control the traffic. Roundabouts enable some sort of self-organization. The configuration of the Magic Roundabout is even more interesting. Unlike regular roundabouts, this one allows various ways to navigate the intersection. It has a higher variety to respond to the variety of not only the traffic density, but also that of the drivers' intentions.

The traffic congestion that Emma entered afterwards is easier to see as the stimuli and responses being out of balance. For that, and elsewhere in the context of the balance, responses should be understood more broadly, not just as reactions, as something that follows the stimuli. Responses in this sense could be developed, installed, prepared, or grown before they are matched against some stimuli. The shell of a turtle protects the turtle from attacks, but it's there even when there is no threat. In the case of a road, it's a matter of its throughput capacity, which depends on how wide it is. When the frequency of new cars increases, it reaches a point when the road cannot absorb the traffic and maintain its desired function, which is to allow travelling at a decent speed. Looked that way, the balance is seen only as between the width of the road and the frequency of passing cars. But that's not the case. The same road with the same frequency of cars that flows smoothly on a sunny day, gets congested when it's raining or when the asphalt needs repair. Variety is a measure which itself has high variety.

Emma compared honking horns with baby cries. Indeed, babies have emotions with higher variety than their means to express them. It's similar with drivers. A honk may want to say many dissimilar things, and often complete opposites, such as "Stop!" and "Move!"

Emma watching the vintage car passing on the other side of the highway, is a simple, and yet very clear, illustration of the balance at work. But it's also an opportunity to see some factors that play a role between the stimuli and responses.

Like any other situation of dealing with the environment, there is an implicit or explicit goal. In fact, it's not one, but a hierarchy of goals where from any position the lower goal looks like the means to achieve the higher goal. The achievement is also dependent on external conditions. When reading a book, we need to be able to distinguish the letters. A lower contrast would make that difficult. That's a condition. But what if it is not a book, but a handwritten letter? There is such a huge variety of scribbled shapes that we need to be able to reduce to the letters in the alphabet so we can read it. Then if we can read the words in the letter okay, it is likely that we also want to understand it. That's not necessarily our ultimate goal. Our ultimate goal may be to have fun or learn something. Understanding is the means to learn or enjoy, but at some level it's a goal in itself. What does it take to achieve it? We need to have the same or higher variety than the text. That means, know the signs, know the words, what they mean by themselves and together in idioms and other contexts. Likewise, if Emma's implicit goal was to follow the movement of the interesting vintage car, then there are some external and internal conditions for that. The external conditions are all the visual obstacles like bushes, car pillars, and water or dirt on the car windows. The internal is the physical ability to follow the movement of the car if nothing obstructs the vision. That includes functioning sight. It also includes unobstructed head movement. And because that morning Emma had a stiff neck, her response to the stimulus of the passing car did not have sufficient variety.

A company environment includes clients, vendors, government, syndicates and, of course, competitors. All these agents do things. Some of these things are relevant to the company in question. It needs to respond to them to remain viable. The new competitor, discussed at the first meeting Emma went to, was obviously threatening or already reducing the market share of the company Emma works for. There are various ways to respond to such stimuli. But all of them can only be successful if their variety is at least as big as the variety of the stimuli. As it seemed that the competitor had offerings not covered by the current product range of Emma's company, one option would be to extend it to match this variety. Covering the demand, combined with better quality, lower price, or in combination with products or services outside the range of the competitor, can be a successful response. The other option – to merge with the competitor – has the same or bigger potential. It is probably the higher variety response. But it's not necessarily the best. Such an increase in variety has a cost.

We keep on living every moment only because we are able to respond successfully to the stimuli of our environment. Our conscious or subconscious responses have more variety than those stimuli that matter for our continuation and for our higher-level goals. In the first couple of hours of one working day, we saw the Law of Requisite Variety ten times in trivial situations. This gives us a huge opportunity to train the habit of using the Stimuli–Responses glasses. Since every hour we can observe how the variety balance works, we can learn and increase the variety of our responses. Once we are able to see how it works when it's obvious, we can hone our skill to recognize it when it's not.

If we can see the variety balance every hour, regardless of the situation we are in, then history should be packed with countless good examples. And indeed, it is. Ever since there was life on the planet, the rise and decline of species, civilizations, nations, cities, and corporations can be seen and better understood with this pair of glasses.

A closer look

Now we are ready to take a closer look at this balance and answer all the initial questions and some new ones too.

Stimuli

What should be regarded as stimuli? In the example we started with, it was the melons, lemons, and cherries thrown at you. They are not stimuli by themselves. They only become such if they matter to you. For the fruit attack, they matter as long as you want to play the game and to the extent of your ambition. What matters in this case is at the conscious level, but other kinds of stimuli, viruses, for example, can matter to you without you being conscious of them.

When reading text, the stimuli are the letters. For reading an analogue clock, it's the position of the two hands, which was what the story of Emma started with. For wiping the phone screen, the stimulus is the dirt on the screen. For adjusting the shower, it is the temperature and the response when trying to regulate it. The weather stimulates in various ways, including the change of temperature, wind speed, sunlight, precipitation, and air pressure. The traffic stimulates a driver by its density and the behaviour of the other participants. A company can be stimulated by a change of the price of a resource, an employee leaving, the bankruptcy of a supplier, a new opportunity, a breakdown of the supply chain, a change of customer preference, a new technology, a change in legislation, and restrictions imposed by the government in crisis situations.

Variety

What we match is not stimuli and responses themselves. We match their variety. In the case of the fruit barrage, the variety of the stimuli depends on the size and shape of the fruit, frequency, speed, and direction of throwing. Sometimes, it's easy to measure variety, like it was for the analogue clock (720) and for the traffic light (eight). In other cases, it's more difficult or simply impossible. The good news is, in most cases we don't need to measure it. We need to see if the variety we have to deal with matches our variety or the variety of our organization. This could be done by a related indicator, such as a drop in sales and stock price, or by a pattern that we can recognize. In fact, we are much better equipped for recognizing patterns than for counting. Let's take a simple example.

Imagine we have a sequence of stimuli made up of the letter *s* repeated at regular intervals. The response to each *s* is the letter *r*. But what if sometimes the response *r* is missing? Then we have a regular sequence of stimuli *s*, with occasional gaps in the sequence of responses *r*.

```
s s s s s s s s s s s s s s s s s s s s s s s s s s s
r r r r r r   r r r r r r r r r r r     r r r r r r r
```

Without having to count, we can immediately see that the variety of the responses doesn't match the variety of the stimuli. By the same token, if a dam wall is functioning, there is no need to measure the variety of the water (counting molecules or measuring pressure) and compare it with the variety of the wall. But if the dam is leaking, we know it doesn't have requisite variety to hold back the water.

A dam is a technology for increasing our variety to manage our water or energy supply. It's part of what makes us human to invent and use tools and technologies to extend variety. And it's usually easy to compare them. For example, it's quite obvious that a gun has more variety than a sword, a dimmer has more variety than a regular light switch, and an Android tablet has more variety than an Egyptian clay tablet. However, if the gun is not loaded, the dimmer is broken, or the battery of the Android tablet is flat, the situation is reversed. But even when the gun is loaded, and both the dimmer and the electronic tablet are functioning, they are useless in the hands of a user who has no clue how they work. In other words, these tools don't extend the variety of such a user, regardless of their potential to do so. The point is that even for simple situations like these, excluding the context can lead us to wrong conclusions. This is all the more pertinent when comparing complex things, such as organizations.

Medium

Remember, we are matching the variety of the stimuli that matter, but we can only respond to those we can register or know about. The variety that we need to match is not necessarily the variety that its source has or is able to generate.

You may have the potential to fully understand a text, but if you read a badly printed copy, you won't be able to match the variety of the text as it comes to you filtered by the medium.

The clock can measure seconds, but we rarely need more than minutes. We are either unable to distinguish anything more precise than that, or we ignore it as unnecessary accuracy. In Emma's story, the confusion did not come from any inability or error on the part of the clock's mechanism. Neither did it come from Emma's inability to read the clock properly. It was the design of the hands that caused the confusion. Overall, this can be seen as a property of the clock. But we can also look at it as a communication problem. As with the bad printout, the medium –

clock hands – did not have the right capacity to transfer the information generated by the clock mechanism to the reader of the clock.

By the same token, watching the vintage car passing, was not only dependent on the speed but also on whether it was a straight section of the road, and if vision was obstructed by fog or bushes. Similarly, honking is not a matter of drivers' inability to formulate a variety of messages. It's just that they are severely limited by their means of communication when driving.

Decision-makers in organizations don't have the capacity to process all the information that matters for the performance of their organization. They use reports and dashboards. These reports and dashboards are filters, and even with the best quality of data and the best intentions, and even though the organizational sensors were able to register it, they often filter out parts of the variety that matter.

Responses

Responses are easy to see and understand, but for this balance, we are interested in their variety. Seeing the variety of the response might be more difficult because doing nothing could be a high-variety response, and this is counterintuitive. One way to make it easier, in the context of the balance, is to imagine three layers of ability to sense and respond: *nature, nurture,* and *now*. The *nature* layer is whatever contributes to variety that is given by nature. When you want to catch fruit thrown your way, you have two hands. They have a specific structure, a particular number of joints, and each movement has a certain limit. If you had two attackers on your left and right, then you'd have an advantage if your eyes were not in front but on the side of your head, like they are for horses and birds.

To some extent, this is changed by the second layer, that of *nurture*. You may train your reflexes and improve your hand–eye coordination.

The actual contribution from *nature* and *nurture* to variety will depend on the way they are used during the period of stimulation. That's the *now* layer.

Not all three layers contribute to variety for everyone and in every situation. Throwing a bottle at a person may smash his face. Throwing a bottle at a tortoise will smash the bottle. In the first case, a trip to the emergency department will happen for sure if left to *nature* but may be avoided with a fast response (*nurture* and *now*). For the tortoise, its variety is only due to *nature*. The other two layers take no part. For organizations, theoretically, the layer of *nature* is missing, although there are things which are difficult to change and as such resemble that layer. Yet, we don't refer to them as *nature*, but as *culture*.

Responses can be conscious. You hear something and decide to turn your head and look in the direction the noise is coming from. Or responses can be outside our control, such as reflexes or hormonal reactions inside our bodies. Organizations also show these two types. In fact, a human unconscious response, "knee-jerk", became a popular classification of some organizational responses.

Organisms respond to what they perceive, but humans and organizations go a step further. Well, much more than a step. When the sun is bright, we put on sunglasses to protect our eyes. But we don't protect them only from irritations that we can register. We use sunglasses with ultraviolet filters, although our bodies don't have sensors to register ultraviolet light. It's a socially determined individual response. It's based on science, technology, our trust in them, and the market forces at play. In any case, we believe that if we don't do it, something bad will happen to us. Companies also respond to stimuli they don't register or create themselves by making predictions for the future.

The three layers of response, *nature, nurture,* and *now* are common for organisms. But humans and their organizations have developed another layer of response not present in other organisms and their organizations. That layer is technology. Technology tremendously increases both our ability to register stimuli and to produce responses with high variety. We can register a signal coming from the other side of the planet and fly to that place in hours.

Balance

An organism or organization can only successfully deal with a situation if the variety of its responses is equal to or bigger than the variety of stimuli that matter. When the demand for your service is increasing rapidly, what can you do to deal with this situation? There are three basic categories of strategies.

One involves increasing your capacity or using some smart technology so that you can absorb the growing variety of your customers.

Another is to change the service to meet the needs of a particular customer group, which might justify increasing the price of the service. Such strategies serve or create a niche market. The variety of the customers will again be absorbed, but not by your business. Those customers outside your target group will go to other service providers. From the perspective of your business, their variety is not absorbed or destroyed, but deflected. Yet, such filtering is a popular way to achieve the balance. Not only niche market strategies, but also setting objectives and management by exception, fall into this category.

The access of environmental variety cannot only be absorbed or deflected, but actually destroyed. This is the third strategy category. Hamsters, for example, eat their babies when there are too many to feed. That may seem cruel to humans, and yet humans destroy other humans in war, in much bigger numbers, and with even poorer justification than that of hamsters.

Such a strategy might not be applicable when the change of environmental variety comes from your customers, but it could be if the change comes from competitors. As long as the competition regulations permit, the variety of a competitor can be literally absorbed by acquisition.

If an organism or organization needs to have requisite variety to succeed in a situation or to adapt to changes in the environment, then it is always successful if its responses have more variety. Why then are we talking about Stimuli–Responses as a balance? The more response variety, the better. Well, not really. Things change when you take into account your energy or resources and when you consider time. A response with much higher variety than that of the stimulus may leave you with insufficient response budget (energy, resource, or time) so that you don't have requisite variety for the next stimulus.

Let's say you are playing a card game with an ace, king, queen, jack ranking. If at the beginning of the game your opponent plays a jack, and you have the choice to absorb the variety of that stimulus by playing either queen or ace, in most games, taking the jack with your ace isn't a wise decision. If you take it with the queen, you can use the extra variety of the ace later in the game, when you may need it.

Risks

When the stimuli have high variety, we can respond in different ways. There are two extreme cases, which need special attention.

One day you get to work, and you have 100 unread emails. For simplicity, let's measure the variety one to one so that the variety of the stimuli is 100. One extreme strategy is to review the subject and sender and classify them as important and not important, not allowing the number of important emails to be more than ten. This way, you reduce the variety of the stimuli to ten. You answer the important ten and delete the rest. Ten for ten, the balance is achieved. However, such a strategy will bear the risk of missing something important or urgent.

In the more general case, classification of stimuli, when allocated to the categories a company is currently equipped to deal with, bears the risk of misclassification. Many stimuli will be of a nature not experienced before, so they won't fit any existing category. They will require a novel response.

The other extreme strategy is to just answer all 100 emails one by one. Here the variety of the response will be 100, so again the balance will be achieved, but this time at a very high cost. The risk is that such an approach may deplete your response resource, leaving you with none for other stimuli.

A successful response should balance between reducing the environmental variety, while managing the risk of misclassifications and oversimplification, and spending too much from the response budget for a high-variety response.

Means

To review the means for achieving variety match, we now need a more precise definition of the Law of Requisite Variety, cast in terms of the Stimuli–Responses balance:

> The variety of the *responses* must be
> equal to or greater than the variety of the *stimuli,*
> divided by the variety of the *goal.*

$$variety\ of\ the\ responses \geq \frac{variety\ of\ the\ stimuli}{variety\ of\ the\ goal}$$

This gives three ways to achieve requisite variety: increase the variety of the responses, reduce the variety of the stimuli, or increase the variety of the goal. And of course, combinations of the three. We'll deal with the variety of the goal later. Now, assuming a constant goal, we can achieve the balance by either reducing external variety or increasing the internal variety. How do we do this?

We reduce external variety by grouping, categorizing, splitting, standardizing, setting objectives, filtering, reporting, coordinating, and consolidating. We can traverse unknown territory by using a map to reduce its variety to that sufficient for navigation. A restaurant may reduce the variety of customers by increasing the quality of service and price, thus attracting only people who can afford and appreciate fine dining.

We increase our variety by learning, trial and error, practising, networking, advertising, buffering, and innovating. A reader can read even a very tiny text by using a magnifying glass. A shoemaker can absorb a higher variety of customers by producing half sizes.

Just as it was with other balances, the level at which we decrease and increase variety matters. A company uses advertising, which is a way to increase its variety, but may be dependent on a well-planned advertising campaign, and planning – used this way – reduces variety.

Some activities are able to both reduce external and increase internal variety. Three of them are especially efficient at that: deciding, planning, and pretending. The first two are common in all organizations, and the third is typical for some organisms. The practice of pretending in organizations has a more general form, which Nils Brunsson calls "organizational hypocrisy". It is a response to getting an increased variety of demands, which are often conflicting. Some demands are answered in words, others in deeds. There is also a more specific form of pretending, where the simultaneous absorption of environmental variety and increase of response variety is done with impressive efficiency and effectiveness. We'll come to this soon.

Decisions are devices that absorb variety by producing one output from many inputs. A decision is making one selection out of several options. This way, the decision reduces their variety to one. Alternatives create uncertainty and decisions kill it.

Once a decision is made, it enables actions and more decisions, which could base themselves on this decision.

Decisions are often disguised. For example, they are hidden inside classifying. Classification of the environmental stimuli is a way to reduce their variety. If we have a 100 different stimuli and group them by similarities into five classes of stimuli, we have reduced their variety 20 times. Classification is a matter of deciding what to put where. If done automatically by some algorithm, there is still a decision to use this algorithm and not another or no algorithm at all.

Planning is also deciding. It is, in fact, a package of decisions about what is to be done, by whom, when, and how. This is how planning reduces variety. But planning also increases it. We get variety increase through planning by being prepared for at least one scenario, especially in the parts we can control, compared to those not prepared even for that. At the same time, we reduce different possibilities to one and try to absorb part of the deflected variety with risk management activities. Often, the increase of variety at one level is successful when variety is decreased at the level below. This point is important, and we'll come back to it later.

Apart from deciding and planning, another activity capable of both increasing and reducing variety is pretending. It has advantages proven by evolution. For many species, pretending means survival. Take, for example, stick insects. The evolutionary pressure to better resemble sticks made them sacrifice their organ symmetry so that they can afford thinner bodies. But why does pretending both decrease external and increase internal variety? Stick insects are not only insects like any other, but also – by their looks – sticks. They resemble a part of a branch of a tree. In a way, they multiply their variety by two, decreasing the perception variety of their predators. A predator sees the stick as a stick and the stick insect as a stick. It doesn't distinguish between the two. Its variety is slashed in half. How advantageous is that? Well, very. Stick insects have been around for 50 million years.

While stick insects pretend to be boring, others pretend to be dangerous. The hoverfly is harmless, but it looks like a bee and predators avoid it.

And mimicking is not a strategy reserved for insects. The very poisonous coral snake is a model for harmless snakes, such as the kingsnake, which evolved to display similar skin patterns.

But if the kingsnake pretends 24/7 with its looks, other snakes pretend only when attacked. The hognose snake, for example, is a real actor. When attacked, the hognose snake goes so far in its act as to stick its tongue out, vomit blood, and sometimes even defecate. That should be not just convincing but quite off-putting even for the hungriest of predators.

Cases like these are impressive and yet, such a combination of simultaneous reducing and increasing of variety is simple enough so that we even have a word for it: pretending. Nowadays, the Stimuli–Responses balance can be kept in such an efficient and effective way using an approach that's much more sophisticated and we still don't have a single word for it. A prime example is the business model of Facebook. The balance is somehow embodied in the enterprise design. The enormous external variety is balanced by … itself. Facebook pumps in external variety. It is a machine for turning stimuli into responses. No matter how many people, interests, and ideas come in, they are met by higher variety. More content emerges out of engagement, which further increases internal variety. But the engagement (that's again responses, likes, and comments) also pays the price for running and expanding the machine. It's paid for by the advertisers, whose variety is met by engagement data, which Facebook owns. And that's the way users pay for the "free" social network service.

So far, we have seen two ways we can achieve the Stimuli–Responses balance by either reducing external variety, that of the stimuli, or increasing the internal variety, that of the responses. Most things we do achieve the one or the other, but there are some that can achieve both.

Let's check the definition of the balance:

$$variety\ of\ the\ responses \geq \frac{variety\ of\ the\ stimuli}{variety\ of\ the\ goal}$$

So, apart from reducing the variety of the stimuli, or increasing the variety of the responses, there is a third way we can influence the balance: we can increase the variety of our goals.

We can see the consequences of ignoring this possibility in the practice of budgeting. Now, budgeting is interesting for being a bad practice, which is at the same time widespread. It is a practice where the external stimuli are not just imbalanced, they are systematically ignored. That's more pronounced nowadays. The rate of change in the environment increases, and yet we keep annual budget cycles and associated incentives, expecting that nothing unexpected will happen for a whole year. But for our purposes, budgeting is interesting for being an area where reducing external and increasing internal variety are not the only ways to keep the balance. We can also change the variety of the goals. It can be reduced by keeping the "number of goals restricted and, wherever possible, not fixed to a point in time", as suggested by Steve Morlidge.

Since stimuli need to be balanced with responses, it may appear that an organization wishes to be stimulated less. That's certainly not the case for all kinds of stimuli, and for some it's just the opposite. Most organizations and notably private companies make a lot of effort to increase certain kinds of stimuli, such as having more customers and markets.

The Essential Balances seen as a variety balance

Now we can put on our new pair of glasses and look at the essential balances in organizations. These three balances, Autonomy–Cohesion, Stability–Diversity, and Exploration–Exploitation already showed some correspondence. Autonomy is somehow related to diversity and exploration. Cohesion is somehow related to stability and exploitation. And here is the key: what they have in common is how they change variety. Autonomy increases it, and so does diversity (in some contexts, it is a synonym of variety). Exploring potentially increases future variety. Respectively, cohesion decreases it, and so does stability. Exploitation potentially decreases future variety. But if we zoom out, each balance, when not maintained, will decrease response variety.

Autonomy and Cohesion

Autonomy increases internal variety. The fruit attack would look very different if your hands were tied behind your back. Or if the fruit thrower had her hands bound together. Removing a constraint, like untying your hands, increases variety right away. Some constraints are obvious, others – such as the social norms we live by – are not, and people may only realize that in extreme situations, like the protagonist in Richard Russo's novel *Straight Man*: "once dignity is surrendered, there are plenty of options".

Let's put on the Stimuli–Responses glasses and look at some of the examples from Chapter 1, "Autonomy and Cohesion". Ferenc responded to the expected variable weather by putting on many layers so he could take off and put on clothes as needed to stay in his zone of comfort. He matched the variability of the weather with the variability of his clothing.

Ferenc had nine tasks that day, six of them with known solutions and independent of others, and for the other three tasks, the solutions were unknown. Let's evaluate the number and uncertainty of stimuli in a simple way, by allocating a point to each task. Let's multiply the points by three if there is a dependency or if the solution is unknown. With these two rules, we'll give all Ferenc's six easy tasks one point each. The other three multiplied by three gives nine, which makes 15 points overall. Let's use this to measure the variety of the stimuli. For the sake of simplicity, we can equate the response to deal with each task with the time needed to complete it. Let's say each point can be done in half an hour, so with a total of 15 points, Ferenc can meet his daily plan in seven and a half hours. If we take this to represent variety, Ferenc's day looked quite well balanced: stimuli with variety 15 can be met by responses with variety 15.

Then the environment changed. A report, which was initially due for the following week, had to be done that day. The variety of the stimuli went up by one, to 16 points. He very likely had a buffer, assuming an eight-hour working day, so he would still be able to absorb the change of variety by using up the remaining half an hour. But then the unexpected one-hour meeting reduced his response budget by two points, bringing it down to 14. The unexpected rule about the method he could use to complete one of the easy tasks revealed his estimation error, so the variety of that task jumped from one point to three in a matter of minutes. In this way, in the course of the day, the 15–15 balance of stimuli and responses, which was in fact, 15–16 counting the buffer, changed to 18–14.

Proper use of technology increases the variety of the user. But when used by many users to achieve a common goal, such an increase of variety can only be achieved if the variety of the individual users is decreased.

The battering ram is a technology which increases variety – it allows us to break down big strong doors that we couldn't without one. But this potential can only be realized if the variety of the users is reduced. The people wielding the battering ram must be coordinated – they must point in one direction and synchronize their movements. This reduction of the autonomy and variety of each person holding the ram is what increases the variety from using it. Only in this way does technology become effective.

Another example of technologies used to conquer fortifications are ladders. Since the height of defensive walls is an important aspect of their variety, then – to have a chance – the attackers' ladders should be of a matching height. But ladders left the assailants exposed, which made them vulnerable to the weapons of the defenders. Siege towers appeared as a solution to that. The trade-off was that they didn't have the portability and flexibility provided by ladders. And then, of course, producing lots of ladders was much faster, cheaper, and easier than producing siege towers. But siege towers had advantages, and they were widely used for many centuries. They are also an easy way to imagine the Stimuli–Responses balance at work: build and put siege towers against defence towers. Match a tower with a tower.

Matching a tower with a tower reminds us of changing the organizational structure to mirror the changes in the environment. We saw that was a source of increased internal complexity in Chapter 2, "Stability and Diversity". We'll diagnose this with the variety balance a bit later. Now, let's look at a few more examples we previously used to illustrate the Autonomy–Cohesion balance, but from the new perspective.

The most important part of the environment of a religious institution are its followers. They have enormous variety. One of the ways it is traditionally reduced is by having a calendar of rituals so that devotees do the same thing, the same way, at the same time. The synchronization cycles are well established and with different granularity. The rituals are fixed, not only for the same time of the year, but also for the same day of the week and time of the day.

By looking at the Autonomy–Cohesion balance with Stimuli–Responses glasses, we can see that the factors and tools for cohesion are factors and tools for reducing both stimuli and responses. The need for safety and the need to reduce uncertainty are *personal* cohesion factors and they are about reducing stimuli, or in other words, about reducing external variety. The *organizational* internal factors for cohesion, such as shared resources, or external factors, such as the temptation of having a single technology supplier, also bring variety down.

Similar logic applies to cohesion tools. Goals, standards, norms, decisions, planning, and coordination are all variety filters. Meetings are coordinated events and as such, they also reduce variety. Just making a meeting possible requires it. We don't meet whenever and wherever each participant wants, but at an agreed time slot and location. But what happens *during* a meeting can not only reduce variety (a decision is made that limits your choice of action), but it may just as well increase it (you present your new idea in front of a big audience).

In summary, the bigger the autonomy of a person or organization, the bigger their repertoire of responses. More cohesion reduces individual responses, but can increase organizational responses and reduce the variety of the stimuli.

Stability and Diversity

The immune system needs to react to the variety of the environmental stimuli – bacteria, viruses, and other invading microorganisms – by generating a matching variety of responses. Such variety has qualitative and quantitative dimensions. The qualitative variety is achieved by the hypermutation. The primary lymphoid organ, the bone marrow, is responsible for generating B cells, the receptors of which have an enormous diversity of shapes. This increases the chance for some of their receptors, the antibodies, to match the shape of antigens. Once the binding is successful, B cells rapidly reproduce at a secondary lymphoid organ (spleen or lymph node), so that the quantity of antibodies can match the quantity of antigens. The variety of antibodies can absorb the variety of antigens only if there is a match with both their qualitative and quantitative dimensions. They must square up in type and in number. Apart from quality and quantity, the timing is also important to achieve the balance. That's why in a lymph node, the dividing B cells produce copies of themselves at a high speed.

When going out, we put on layers of clothes to match the variability of the weather. When we are at home, our air conditioning systems use thermostats to make sure the temperature inside stays the same even when the outside temperature changes. Bees don't have clothes and thermostats, but they have their own way of regulating the temperature of their hives. The differences between individual bees give the requisite variety of the beehive to respond to changes in the weather. Individual bees start buzzing or fanning at different times, so the beehive temperature changes smoothly.

The yield of Peruvian potato farmers depended heavily on the weather. And there were other environmental hazards, such as insect blight and stealing. Not being able to predict the external stimuli, the potato farmers in Peru kept their strips of land scattered so that their risk exposure varied. The goal was to avoid starvation. Having some yield each year was better than risking years with no crop at all. Keeping more than ten scattered strips of land was their way of having sufficient variety to absorb the variety of the hazards.

Diversifying in the face of the unknown is widespread wisdom. "Don't put all your eggs in one basket." And it is well known in business, where companies diversify their investment, product, and service portfolios. The same conviction isn't necessarily applied when hiring diverse people. It's more often a matter of compliance or for attracting customers who are sensitive to this topic. And indeed, organizations hiring diverse people may experience difficulties in times of stability, but it is a way to increase the variety of their responses in times of change and uncertainty. Any kind of diversity, such as those of gender, ethnicity, age, disability, as well as different relationships, not necessarily related to immediate work necessity, can increase response variety.

Internal diversity may also reduce variety. How could that be? When an organization diversifies its structure in response to regulatory change, competition, or a new technology trend, this increases internal complexity. Disagreement also increases. There are more and different needs that have to be met. More communication channels are now needed, and more coherence due to a redistribution of power to multiple centres with little alignment. The organization has to deal with these challenges. No matter how it's done, this uses up a big part of their response variety.

Companies tend to reduce their response variety, not only in times of change, but also in times of stability. Whatever is not contributing directly to the current way of working is regarded as redundant, unnecessary, and inefficient. Some of it really is. Yet, cutting it all makes them vulnerable in times of environmental change. When there is no need of high response variety, it's more efficient to reduce it, but it can't be restored quickly when taken by surprise. In other words, long periods of successful maintenance of the Stimuli–Responses balance reduces the variety of the response.

Exploration and Exploitation

Exploration (potentially) increases future variety. It does so by discovering currently unknown sources of energy, solutions to current and future problems, new working methods for better efficiency, new markets, and new business models. While exploration is a way to better prepare for the future, exploitation provides resources to ensure current viability. Over-exploring reduces the current variety of response, which in extreme cases will make the potential variety gain useless because the organization may not exist at the time it could have used that latent variety. Respectively, over-exploiting may either deplete the current response resource, or may leave the organization with insufficient variety to meet environmental changes in the future.

Dismissing jazz festivals with unknown musicians is like treating potential information as noise. If jazz musicians themselves don't venture to experiment, both on and off stage, they won't be successful. Miles Davis disrupted his band by calling unrehearsed songs and familiar songs in new keys. But getting that level of variety takes not only courage to experiment, but also the will to resist the attraction and comfort of exploitation. "Do you know why I don't play ballads anymore?" Miles Davis once asked Keith Jarrett. "Because I like to play ballads so much."

Before it evaporates, the pheromone trail helps ants to exploit discovered sources of food. Then they can explore and discover new sources. The pheromone trail works to amplify their variety to match that of the discovered forage. Normally many ants are needed to exploit it. If the pile is divided by the carrying capacity of each ant, then we can take this as a way to measure the variety of the stimuli. The response variety will match it if enough ants know where the forage is. They inform each other by leaving pheromone trails. The more ants carry a piece of food to the nest, the fresher the pheromone trail, which recruits even more ants and leads them to the source. This way of gaining variety to match quantity is similar to the B cells. When the B cells' antibodies better match the shape of the antigens, they produce more copies of themselves.

But then if too many ants follow and leave pheromone trails, there will be no discoveries of new sources of food. As the rambling will be largely inefficient, there needs to be many exploring ants to increase the chance of some of them finding something. This is another similarity with the B cells. The high rate of mutation of B cells increases the chance of some of them "recognizing" the pathogens.

In terms of the Exploration–Exploitation balance, the pheromone trail increases exploitation. In terms of the Autonomy–Cohesion balance, it's a constraint enabling coordination. It brings increased cohesion. In terms of Stimuli–Responses, the current response variety is increased, but if that goes too far it eats up the variety for future responses. Thinking in terms of variety helps not only our understanding of what we put on each plate of the balancing scale, but how the balance itself works.

Then why don't we use only the Stimuli–Responses glasses? There are specific features of each of the essential balances for which variety is sometimes too abstract to help in diagnosis and design.

Now, let's take another look at a previous example of the Exploration–Exploitation balance through the Stimuli–Responses lens.

A new employee who is a quick learner will have sufficient variety to promptly absorb that part of the organizational variety which matters for the job. She will blend in and will soon start bringing value. But a slow learner may be able to contribute to organization response variety by questioning established norms, by being conservative about fads otherwise embraced by the company culture, and by coming up with foreign ideas when the company fails to meet challenges with its habitual range of responses.

The pattern we see so far is that both exploration and exploitation add variety. Exploration now can increase variety in the future, while exploitation now does it now. But exploitation now can also raise variety in the future by increasing the response budget. And sometimes exploration can also generate variety in the present. Here's an example.

A competitor has a new release of their software packed with cool features, which attract some of your clients to switch. You bring down the variety of the response with a proper analysis and based on that you increase your variety by adding the same features, plus something extra (lower price, a more flexible licence, nicer interface, even more features, or a stripped-down free version) to compensate for being late. This way of getting requisite variety is exploitation. But what if you misclassified the stimuli, and it turned out it wasn't just a matter of an app having new features, or a new app appearing on the market? What if that was only the tip of the iceberg, the prominent part of an entirely new business model? In that case, both the attempts to reduce the variety of the stimuli and increase your own variety should involve a lot of trial and error and a lot of exploration.

Looking at various situations with the pair of glasses of an essential balance and that of the Stimuli–Responses showed that in all situations the latter works. But more importantly, whenever there is an organization, all three essential balances and the meta-balance are there. We can also observe this in everyday situations, for example, when children are playing.

When two kids engage in make-believe play, an organization emerges. But it is a different organization than the one arising between two adults in a narrow corridor. It happens not in spite but because of the activities of the two kids and it lasts longer, as long as they want and are able to maintain it. In a way, the kids are in full control. They not only create the organization, but also its environment. They complement whatever they find that resembles something and create the stimuli they then respond to with different levels of success due to constraints created again by them. They have the autonomy to choose a flat stone to resemble a car, but this new reality can only be maintained by the way they use their hands to move the stone on the ground and make it sound. In doing so they have started to impose constraints. Each of the kids can lift the stone off the ground easily, but then it would no longer be a car but perhaps a plane, or a bird. So they won't do it as long as they want to maintain the role of the stone as a car. And that constraint is not enough. They invent other rules on the basis of what they were able to achieve previously. Rules are important. Without rules and constraints, the make-believe play will be random and boring; it will lack cohesion and will disintegrate. Keeping the game in the fun zone also needs the balance between stability and diversity. The participants should behave as expected, the rituals should be repeated, and all the comfort of known things used. But importantly, there should also be new situations and surprises to keep the make-believe organization enjoyable. Yet, the current rules have limited potential, which gets exhausted, and at some point the play risks no longer being entertaining. The fun resources of the territory demarcated by the current rules are fully exploited, and other territories need to be explored to change the make-believe and bring it back in the fun zone, between new and old and between too difficult and too easy.

The three essential balances and the generic variety balance are useful for diagnosing and designing organizations separately and even more beneficial when applied in combination. We saw how potent combining or overlaying these perspectives can be. It can be even more powerful still. Such combinations enable seeing other important balances by lifting the fog of the organizational culture and ideology. The culture fog makes it difficult to see what's going on when the current way of doing business doesn't work. Organizations are prone to forget and to repeat mistakes. Often, there is not even the right language to discuss the hot problems with.

One such balance, enabled by the Stimuli–Responses glasses, will be described in the following section.

Requisite inefficiency

Organizations are constantly pressed to increase their efficiency. To do more with less. To make rational, well-justified decisions. To make things faster, cheaper, and to get rid of whatever brings no value. To carefully analyze what works best and specialize so that they get better at it. Yet striving for efficiency comes with a risk. It makes organizations inflexible. When the environment changes, their responses lack variety to meet the new stimuli. They are trained to be good in circumstances which no longer exist. It turns out that some inefficiency is not necessarily bad. It is, in fact, a precondition for survival.

If we put the Stimuli–Responses glasses on, we see that the variety of the response of an organism or an organization needs to be at least equal to the variety of the external stimulus in order to deal with it. What happens when a stimulus has higher variety than that of the current response? Then that organism or organization has to reduce the stimulus variety and / or increase its own. And do it fast. This is where we have to consider another important factor: time. The question now is: If the organization can muster the needed variety, can it do it before it's too late? Or, more to the point, what would increase its chances of producing the missing variety in a short time? The answer is, it needs some reserve of variety, adaptive flexibility, randomness, and sometimes simply luck.

Both individuals and organizations have established standard ways to manage risk, in other words, to prepare for something negative happening that leads to injury, loss, or some other kind of damage. Such methods are contingency planning, reserve funds, insurance, spare production capacity, and failover clustering, to name just a few. It is indeed the case of having reserve variety. None of this variety (or response budget to ramp up variety when needed) is used if nothing bad happens and most parts keep functioning as expected. These buffers are related to uncertainty, but to an expected one. We don't know what will happen, yet when it does, we can classify it as technology failure, fire, flood, transport accident, earthquake, hurricane, or extremely bad weather. We can put a name and assign some probability to it, because such things are known to happen. We are historically prepared to expect them.

Yet, none of these reserves and backup strategies can be considered as "inefficient". It's only when the risk strategy goes a step further that it could look inefficient, as was the case with the Peruvian potato farmers.

It gets even more inefficient when there is randomness. And we saw a lot of it with ants rambling aimlessly around, and with the hypermutation of B cells, most of which are useless and simply die. But one of the wandering ants may stumble upon a new source of food and will summon others to gather it. And the receptors of a particular B cell may match those of a pathogen and start reproducing to mark them all for elimination. Every situation of complete uncertainty can only be handled if there is the ability to generate random responses.

Redundancy

There are several "inefficient" strategies that have proved evolutionarily successful. One is the reserve of variety, a good example of which is genetic redundancy. Some genes having the same function are duplicated, so that if there is a mutation in one of them, the other can successfully carry out that function. We have established similar strategies in life. We keep a spare tyre in our cars. When the main server goes down, we have mechanisms to automatically switch to a spare application server to ensure service continuity. This is functional redundancy. It means there are two or more components of the *same* kind which are able to perform the *same* function and in normal operations the spare ones are passive.

Temporary shift of function

Another inefficient but highly effective way to prepare for risks and uncertainty is to have *different* components performing the *same* functions when needed. In biology this phenomenon is called *degeneracy*. It is observed with genes, proteins, and metabolism. We have instances of this in society, for example, when the army is mobilized to help in times of disasters, such as floods and earthquakes. In some cities there are taxis and fire trucks rigged out with basic paramedic equipment. Their drivers are trained to provide first aid. These taxis and fire trucks can shift their function and serve as ambulances when needed. Following similar logic, some organizations tend to hire people with so-called T-shaped profiles. Such people have deep knowledge in a certain area and some good knowledge in a number of other areas. Although the motivation is to facilitate collaboration between different disciplines at work, it also works as a temporary shift of function. Shift of function, however, is actually expected in Agile development, and the success of these practices spread them outside software production.

If we zoom in to the case of a shift of function, we can see that some of them are based on the history of events. There is a specialization, a readiness to carry out a specific additional function. In other words, it is a prepared shift of function for an expected kind of adverse event. These are not helpful when there is completely unexpected change in the environment or when the effects of a known kind of event have not been experienced in recent times. The spread of Covid-19 showed that very clearly. Some organizations were able to meet the unexpected stimuli with novel responses while others relied on routine business continuity practices, most of which turned out to be inadequate.

Permanent shift of function

A shift of function can be for a long period, complementing or completely replacing the initial function. In evolutionary studies, this is called *exaptation.* A classic example is bird feathers. Their initial function was temperature regulation. Birds used their feathers to trap air when cold. When it was too warm, by lifting up their feathers, they were able to cool their bodies. Then feathers evolved for insect catching, sexual display, and finally for flight. An excellent fit for flight does not prevent exaptation for other functions.

Another example of exaptation is the lungs of some basal fish, which evolved for buoyancy control. A third example is in mammals, where some of the jawbones abandoned their initial function and evolved to improve hearing. Even when the mechanisms of natural selection are created artificially (e.g. using genetic algorithms), the most successful strategy can use exaptation and show short-term inefficiency.

Similar examples can be seen not only in the evolution of species but also in the evolution of technology. Maybe the most popular one is the discovery of the microwave oven. In 1945, a chocolate bar, in the pocket of Percy Spencer at Raytheon, started to melt when it was exposed to the microwaves from an active radar set.

In biological exaptation an organ adopts a new function, abandoning its initial one, in most cases. In technology exaptation, discovering a new function does not lead to abandoning the initial one if it's still useful, thus increasing the individual and collective variety of humans even more.

In most cases, such discoveries are serendipitous. Apart from the microwave, the discoveries of Teflon, nylon, penicillin, aspartame, among others, are due to serendipity. Importantly, this is not simply chance and luck. It requires allowing accidental things to happen and being prepared to make sense of the unexpected.

Rationalization and efficiency are based on what has happened in the past and what is anticipated or planned for the future. According to the Stimuli–Responses balance, to respond to the unexpected or uncertainty from outside, we should have a way to allow uncertainty inside. We should design our organizations for serendipity. Allowing diversity of people, including misfits and slow learners, as we saw through Exploration–Exploitation glasses in the previous chapter, is what brings the conditions to gain internal variety quickly when something unexpected and significant happens. As there might be nothing from the past or the projected future that would justify such a design, it will appear inefficient and irrational. But there is a requisite inefficiency which shouldn't be just tolerated. It must be actively maintained. It is seemingly unnecessary perspectives that could save the day in unforeseen future situations. It is unjustified collaboration that may create the conditions for innovation. The requisite inefficiency may appear in the form of functional redundancy, degeneracy, or creating conditions for serendipity and exaptation. And it may be in entirely novel forms that could not be captured in any of these currently known categories.

Since some inefficiency is needed when there is uncertainty, then more inefficiency is requisite when the uncertainty is high. However, in times of crisis or uncertainty, the natural response is to reduce the overall inefficiency, and with it, the part that might be what the organization or society needs to survive the crisis.

Summary

In order to succeed in a particular situation and to survive in the long run, the responses of an organism or organization should have more variety than the challenges of the environment. Variety is a measure of complexity, as introduced by Ross Ashby. While in everyday language we use variety as a synonym of diversity, in Ashby's Law of Requisite Variety it combines those aspects of the stimuli and responses that are meaningful for the outcome.

If fruits are thrown at you, their number, frequency, and size will determine the variety of the stimuli. Your capacity and the agility of your catching devices will limit the variety of your responses. When reading a text, the variety of the text is shaped by the number of different letters and by the meanings of words and idioms. For a company, the variety of the stimuli may depend on the number of its clients, their taste, preferences, age groups, income, locations, and behaviour.

When the Law of Requisite Variety is recast in terms of the Stimuli–Responses balance, it states that:

> The variety of the *responses* must be
> equal to or greater than the variety of the *stimuli*,
> divided by the variety of the *goal*.

With Stimuli–Responses glasses on, we can see that letters when reading, dirt when cleaning, the weather forecast when deciding what to wear, and traffic density when driving, are all regular stimuli we need to respond to in our everyday life. A company can be stimulated by a price surge of a product ingredient, an employee leaving, the bankruptcy of a supplier, a new opportunity, a change of customer preference, a new technology, or changing legislation. It may respond by investing in research for an alternative formula to avoid the expensive ingredient, recruiting an employee, contacting another supplier, seizing the opportunity, adopting the new technology, and taking measures to be compliant with the new regulation, respectively, or in other ways.

To respond effectively to stimuli, organisms or organizations must be able to detect them. That depends both on their perception and on what stands between them and the source of the stimuli. There are stimuli that an organization is not able to detect or that it just misinterprets.

The variety of response of organizations depends on their culture, their adaptive capability, the context when selecting a particular response, and on how they use technologies.

There are three ways to achieve Stimuli–Responses balance. The first is to reduce the variety of the stimuli. A restaurant may reduce the variety of customers by increasing the quality of service and price, thus attracting only people who can afford and appreciate fine dining. Typical ways to reduce external variety involve grouping, categorizing, splitting, standardizing, setting objectives, filtering, reporting, coordinating, and consolidating. The main risk with this strategy is oversimplification. Once a certain stimulus is classified, for example, a competitive service that has an extra feature attracting people, this may result in looking for a response belonging to the corresponding class of responses, such as investing in a similar feature. But it may happen that what attracts the customers is not so much that feature, but an entirely different business model for which there is no appropriate classification so far.

The second way to achieve the balance is to increase the variety of the responses. When a restaurant faces a surge in demand for its service, it may respond by enlarging the premises, hiring more personnel, diversifying the menu, or introducing electronic ordering online or on the premises. More generally, the variety of responses is increased by learning, trial and error, practising, networking, advertising, buffering, and innovating. The risk here is using up the whole response budget to produce matching variety, so it's always wiser to combine this strategy with the one for reducing the stimuli.

The third way to achieve balance between stimuli and responses is by increasing the variety of the goal.

Often the three types of strategies are combined. For example, planning, deciding, and pretending decrease the variety of the stimuli while increasing the variety of the response at the same time. And if our restaurant does not increase its capacity or prices, but instead starts accepting customers by reservation only, this is a combination of decreasing the variety of the stimuli and increasing the variety of the goal. The variety of the goal is increased by accepting that any number of potential customers over the capacity will not be served by that restaurant.

But there are even smarter ways to achieve the balance by pumping in external variety so that the capacity to produce requisite variety grows naturally. And growth is only possible if you are able to increase the desired kind of stimuli (customers), while finding a way to generate a matching variety of responses.

The situations we looked at with the glasses of the three essential organizational balances can be interpreted through the lens of Stimuli–Responses. Autonomy and diversity increase response variety, but also the potential to come up with new ideas for reducing the variety of stimuli. Exploring potentially increases future variety. Cohesion decreases variety and so does stability. Exploitation potentially decreases future variety. If we zoom out, each balance, when not maintained, will decrease response variety.

To get requisite variety when needed means tolerating some inefficiencies at all times. When organizations optimize their resources, they do so for the current circumstances. But when the environment changes, their responses lack the variety to meet the new stimuli. They are trained to be good in circumstances which are no longer present. It turns out that some inefficiency is not just desired, it is, in fact, a precondition for survival. The inefficiency may be in the form of redundancy or a shift of function, which may be temporary or permanent.

Now we have four pairs of glasses, three for the essential balances and one universal pair which can be used on its own or to enhance the lenses of the other three. Autonomy and cohesion, stability and diversity, and exploration and exploitation, they all represent dilemmas, tensions between alternatives. But these alternatives can be balanced. There is a solution. The relationships of some alternatives are such that there is no solution. Each points to itself through the other. Such situations we call paradoxes. They are more difficult to understand and work with than the tensions, which can be balanced. Yet, it turns out that, with the right pair of glasses, we can see that paradoxes are not simply widespread in organizations, in fact, organizations are made out of paradoxes and exist thanks to paradoxes. Such a pair of glasses is more difficult to use, but if you have reached this far, you are ready for the last chapter.

NOTES

1. [Imagine] three layers of ability to sense and respond: *nature, nurture,* and *now*.

Such a split between stimuli and responses is useful due to its simplicity, but that comes at a price, especially when applied to organisms. It feels like the responses come after the stimuli and that somehow the ability to register stimuli (perception) is of different nature and separated from the ability to respond (action). In fact, perception and action are intertwined, and action, as well as the body plan of an animal, plays an important role in perception. And then although looking at the ability to sense and respond in layers of *nature, nurture,* and *now* is very pragmatic, when a more rigorous one is needed, it's worth checking the dynamical-systems account of sensorimotor contingencies proposed by Buhrmann et al. (Buhrmann, Di Paolo, & Barandiaran, 2013). They distinguish sensorimotor environment, sensorimotor habitat, sensorimotor coordination, and sensorimotor strategies. The latter are also referred to as "schemes" in Di Paolo, Cuffari, and De Jaegher

(2018). If and how such a classification can be applied to organizations is an open question.

2. If you had two attackers on your left and right, then you'd have an advantage if your eyes were not in front but on the side of your head, like they are for horses and birds.

The advantage of a panoramic view, however, comes at the expense of depth perception and night vision.

3. Throwing a bottle at a tortoise will smash the bottle.

There are authors who prefer to distinguish this part of the response arsenal as separate constant (Aulin-Ahmavaara, 1979), and some refer to that as "buffering". Aulin's modification of the Law of Requisite Variety looks like this:

$$H(Y) \geq H(D) + H_D(R) - H(R) - K$$

Where, H(Y) is the variety of the outcome (in fact, Aulin uses "entropy" as a measure of a variety), H(D) is the variety of the disturbance, $H_D(R)$ is the uncertainty involved in the acts of the regulator, H(R) is the variety of the regulatory acts, and K is a "possible constant reduction" (ibid.), which Heylighen refers to as "buffering" (Heylighen & Joslyn, 2001).

4. [W]hile managing the risk of misclassifications and oversimplification, and spending too much from the response budget for a high-variety response.

For a detailed discussion on this topic, see Boisot and McKelvey (2011).

5. We increase our variety by learning, trial and error, practising, networking, advertising, buffering, and innovating.

Technology is not included, as it can be used for both increasing the response variety and reducing the variety of the stimuli. It can also be described as something which increases our "adaptive frontier" (Boisot & McKelvey, 2011). Boisot and McKelvey introduce the Ashby Space, where the vertical axis shows the variety of the stimuli and the horizontal axis shows the variety of the responses. In that Ashby Space, they define the "adaptive frontier", beyond which there is no budget for adaptation (ibid.).

6. The practice of pretending in organizations has a more general form, which Nils Brunsson calls "organizational hypocrisy".

Organizations are subject to conflicting demands from clients, employees, society, and regulators. Stakeholders react not only to organizational actions but also to organizational announcements and decisions. This enables organizations to "meet some demands through talk, others through its decisions, and yet others through action—and thus to some extent, satisfy three conflicting demands" (Brunsson, 2007). Organizational hypocrisy as "a way of handling conflicts by reflecting them in inconsistencies among talk, decisions, and actions" (ibid.).

7. Alternatives create uncertainty and decisions kill it.

These alternatives are not pregiven, and neither do they appear by themselves. There is a sort of decision in the form of conscious or unconscious selection, even before the decision. This is the selection that reduces the possible options to those considered as input by the decision.

8. The evolutionary pressure to better resemble sticks made them sacrifice their organ symmetry so that they can afford thinner bodies.

See Trivers (2014).

9. It's paid for by the advertisers, whose variety is met by engagement data, which Facebook owns.

The short-circuiting of supply and demand of variety causes a massive reduction of information variety on the web. Facebook is addictive. People spend a lot of time there turning it into a single information provider. The World Wide Web is designed as a highly decentralized system that gives the incredible opportunity to use many independent information sources at no cost, so users can compare, complement, and validate. Facebook turns the web into a highly centralized system replacing the natural variety with a world created by algorithms. They aim at keeping the users there longer, which feeds the algorithms with more data that further improves them.

10. It can be reduced by keeping the "number of goals restricted and, wherever possible, not fixed to a point in time".

See Morlidge (2017).

11. Then the environment changed.

Environment is relative; it's always an environment *of*. The systems in focus here, unlike machines, for example, are such that they have self-asserted identity and as long as they live they actively maintain a distinction between themselves and their environment. For Ferenc, the work environment includes people and teams he interacts with. If his work is client-facing, then clients will also be part of his environment, which will be an overlap between his work environment and the environment of the organization he works for. See also the section "Boundary" in the "Productive Paradoxes" chapter.

12. But siege towers had advantages, and they were widely used for many centuries.

See Campbell (2006).

13. Miles Davis disrupted his band by calling unrehearsed songs and familiar songs in new keys.

See Barrett (1998).

14. An excellent fit for flight does not prevent exaptation for other functions.

Exaptation is a term proposed by Stephen Jay Gould and Elisabeth Vrba in 1982 (Gould & Vrba, 1982). When tracing the evolution of feathers, from fitting the function of temperature regulation to finally evolving for flight, the authors also point to contemporary cases, such as the Black Heron of Africa, which uses its wings to make a shadow in order to better see small fish in shallow waters (McLachlan & Liversidge, 1978).

15. A third example is in mammals, where some of the jaw bones abandoned their initial function and evolved to improve hearing.

See Allin (1975).

16. Even when the mechanisms of natural selection are created artificially (e.g. using genetic algorithms), the most successful strategy can use exaptation and show short-term inefficiency.

Melanie Mitchell described an experiment with a simple robot whose strategy evolved on the basis of a genetic algorithm (Mitchell, 2011). The robot has to clean a grid of empty soda cans, where each square can either be empty or contain a soda can. The robot has no memory and can only see the content of adjacent cells. Interestingly, the most successful strategy involved not picking up a soda can while in a cell with one (short-term inefficiency), but using it as breadcrumb instead, as external memory (exaptation).

17. Maybe the most popular one is the discovery of the microwave oven.

See *Technology Review* (1999).

18. It is seemingly unnecessary perspectives that could save the day in unforeseen future situations.

The SAGE Handbook of Complexity and Management brings various perspectives from the studies of complexity that are relevant for management, but one of the common conclusions is that the future survival and success of organizations is dependent on "the tolerance of, and ultimately organizational understanding of, seemingly unnecessary perspectives, views, and ideas" (Merali & Allen, 2011).

5

PRODUCTIVE PARADOXES

Only those questions which are in principle undecidable, we can decide.

— Heinz von Foerster

All the previous chapters described ways to diagnose and design organizations by recognizing and analyzing factors and means to maintain a few essential balances. These perspectives were provided by metaphorical pairs of glasses. Choosing glasses over lens is not accidental. Glasses have frames. Frames serve as a constant reminder that every perspective has limitations, creates a bias, and leaves a blind spot. Using the same glasses might be problematic in some situations or in all situations if we wear them for too long. We should take off the glasses of one balance and put on a pair of another balance. But sometimes, we need a completely new pair of glasses. Through its lenses we might see organizations not as nested balances but as something else.

Using new pairs of glasses doesn't just complement but also confirms the thinking habits from the previous pairs. In fact, using only the balances is rather extreme and not balanced. So, paradoxically, to have a balance, using balancing glasses should be balanced with using other kinds of glasses. And paradoxes, contrary to what our thought tradition teaches us, are not necessarily to be avoided. It might be that they are not logical errors but something natural, even essential for organizations. This is what the new pair of glasses is about. And, as it happens, the glasses we'll try on during this chapter will point to wearing balancing glasses again, either those you are have learned about so far, or new ones.

I named the new glasses "Productive Organizational Paradoxes" (POP). After trying out and designing different pairs of glasses, I found this one particularly useful and insightful. But it's not very easy to get used to them.

I remember the first week with my current pair of actual, not metaphorical, glasses. I bought the glasses from a shop in Antwerp. The owner offered a new kind of lenses, which while serving their main function to correct near-sightedness, also delay the inevitable onset of far-sightedness. Their usefulness came at double the price. One was the price in euros and the other was the initial discomfort. In the first week, I had headaches and difficulties when driving. Quite often that new pair of glasses brought me a sort of dizziness. This might also happen when you start wearing the POP glasses. You might get dizzy for a while, but it's worth making some effort to overcome this period. The POP glasses have great explanatory power, although they are certainly not easy eyewear.

The design of the POP glasses is inspired by and based on the social theory of Niklas Luhmann. This will require clarification of some concepts, which, while widely used in everyday life, should be treated with more precision. I'll avoid going deep into theoretical exposition and limit myself to the minimum needed for successful use in practice.

Boundary

Boundary is a powerful concept. It is not sufficiently understood and appreciated. Do you know, for example, that you can base most of mathematics not on numbers but only on the concept of boundary? If we add 2 and 3, because of what we are taught in school, we say it's 5. These symbols stand for something. But "5" doesn't look like "2", nor like "3". We need to map things to symbols they stand for. It is much more natural to see adding as putting things together. Putting things together doesn't change what things look like. And then the arithmetical operation is a matter of drawing and removing boundaries. If you put stones on the sand and you separate them by drawing a line, this is subtraction. If you remove the line, it's addition. Multiplication and division are achieved by nesting boundaries.

However, these operations depend on other invisible boundaries that we make when we see things. We know what a stone looks like. We can distinguish it from its background. This distinction is the first boundary. It is we who know and distinguish what a stone looks like and then create another boundary so that we have two groups of stones. Unlike stones, organisms and organizations create their boundaries themselves.

As it is our tradition so far, we'll look at organisms first and then move to organizations. For an organism, there should be a way to say where it ends and where its environment starts. There should be some boundary. And if we take a human or a snake, we can say that the boundary is the skin. There is something material which wraps up an organism so that we can speak of inside and outside. But an organism is an organism when it is alive. When it is dead, the skin, or whatever is on the surface of its body, is no longer a boundary. A dead organism can't feel or do things. It is no longer separated from its environment. In fact, we can't speak anymore of organism and environment. When the organism is dead, they both disappear.

This means that neither the particular substance nor structures are what makes an organism what it is when it is alive. What makes it alive is that it produces itself every moment, it reproduces itself. We are going to use "reproduces" here only in the sense of continuous self-production, not in the sense of producing offspring of any kind. But how does this reproduction happen? Let's look at a single cell.

There are various chemical reactions in the cell which are linked to each other so that they form a closed network. Every reaction, every process, depends on some other internal process. Of course, they also depend on energy and resources coming from the environment. But it is the closed network of processes that makes the difference between organisms and environment. In the case of the cell, its semipermeable membrane looks like a boundary. But this membrane is produced by internal chemical reactions, which the membrane itself makes possible. If it wasn't there, the chemicals would be dispersed and not enter into the reactions that produce the components of the cell. At the same time, it is these reactions, and not anything external, that produce the membrane that enables them. This is how the cell produces the boundary so that there is the inside of the cell and the outside. The boundary is produced internally, and it itself enables its own production. The cell is at the same time closed and open. Only by being closed is it open to get the raw materials it needs to continue its reproduction and maintain its closure.

The reproduction and the closure are not only at the level of the cell. It also happens at the next level. The immune system, for example, is able to make a boundary by creating a closed network of cells. By maintaining this boundary, the immune system is able to function.

It is similar with organizations. They create and maintain their own boundary internally. But instead of chemical processes and cells, their closed network is made up of communications.

Communications

Communications in organizations need four elements to happen. If one of them is missing, it's not an organizational communication. The first is the utterance, the announcement. It could be oral, written, or it could be a video message. And then it should be meaningful for somebody. This is the second requisite element. The utterance is about *how* the message is produced and *that* a message is produced, and even *why* a message is produced. The meaning is about the *what*, and not the *how* and the *why*. Two messages, received by different channels and in different ways, can be interpreted as having the same meaning. Also, different messages can be uttered in the same way but have different meanings in different contexts.

The third element of communication is information. A message can be uttered, can be understood, and still not represent information. How so? Well, although we use information daily, here we need more precision: information is something that is new, something that makes a difference – again the importance of boundary.

To inform means to let somebody know. Ferenc didn't know about the meeting at two o'clock. He then received a mail (announcement), understood it, and was informed about the meeting. If he were to receive another mail also telling him about the meeting at two, he would recognize the fact that it was a new message, and he'd understand its meaning. But that message wouldn't carry information to him, as he already knows about the meeting at two. He is already *in*formed. Now, if after the first message, he had forgotten about the meeting, then it would be information again. Information is what makes the difference.

The fourth element is reference. It's sort of active understanding, but not by people, by following communications. A communication participates in the ongoing reproduction of an organization if it refers to previous, and is referred to by following, communications.

When we see organizations through POP glasses, what keeps them alive, by creating a boundary between them and their environment, is not a set of separate communications, but communications that refer to each other and in doing so, form a closed network. With such a closed network of communications, other functional domains of society, such as education, science, and economics also reproduce themselves. Organizations are different in that they are made up of a specific type of communications: decisions.

Decisions

When Ferenc decided what to wear that day, that's not a decision that participates in the organization he works for. Making decisions on work-related matters is still irrelevant for the organization until they are communicated with reference to a previous internal decision. Even then, there needs to be a future decision that refers to it. Otherwise, the current decision simply disappears as organizational noise.

When decisions are uttered and understood, they are always already information as they bring something new, they make a difference. The situation is not the same after the decision is made.

We all know decisions of type "Catch-22", which are paradoxical. However, what may come as a shock is that when organizations are looked at through POP lens, all decisions are paradoxical.

Paradox is commonly used to name a range of things, from dilemmas and tensions (such as our balances) to circular references.

Here, by *paradox*, we mean only the latter. The classic example is: "This statement is false." It is a paradox because it is a statement about itself. It refers to itself. Any attempt to solve it produces a contradiction. As it's not meaningless, it must be either true or false. If it is true, then it must be false, as it states. But if it is false, then saying that it is false makes it true.

It is obvious to see the paradox in this sentence, but not so when it comes to decisions. And yet, they are not just paradoxical, but keep appearing so when looked at from different angles.

"Only *those* questions which are in principle undecidable, *we* can decide," as Heinz von Foerster put it. And indeed, we don't decide what the sum of 2 and 3 is. In computational terms, it is a "decidable" problem, one that has a solution. All we have to do is to calculate it to get the result. Or more generally, we are able to apply a rule which will produce the result. It could be generally accepted conventions (axioms, for example), or more specific conventions, such as the banks' "Rule of 78". Both situations, calculation and application of a rule, are based on past decisions but are by nature decidable in the sense of having a non-arbitrary result got by following an agreed logic.

That's not the case with the situation that Emma faced in her first meeting of the day. The issue of the new competitor demanded a reaction, and such a reaction could not be produced by calculation. They discussed whether to increase their product range to cover what the competitor sells well, or to merge with the competitor. There is a choice that needed to be made. Also note that to nominate these two particular options is also a matter of decisions.

If the decision is to merge with the competitor, it also communicates its alternatives. And here we see another inherent paradox. A decision communicates both its alternative and the fact that it is not its alternative. If the decision for the acquisition was taken and communicated, such communication also communicates, explicitly or implicitly, that something else could have been decided instead, such as to increase the product range and to cover what the competitor sells well. In other words, if it can't communicate its alternatives, then it wasn't a decision but something inevitable. But if it can't communicate that it is not its alternative, that would mean that nothing was decided. The specific property of a decision to both communicate its alternatives and that it is not its alternatives, makes it possible for decisions to be criticized, blamed, and regretted.

The most important function of decisions is to absorb uncertainty. Several or many options are available (in fact, created) before a decision is made. The selection is unknown. Until a choice is made, the uncertainty is high because different futures are anticipated as a consequence of each choice. In terms of the Stimuli–Responses balance, there is high variety. Decisions then are a variety reduction device, or rather, a variety displacement device.

Once a decision is made, it enables new decisions to be based on it. This produces other paradoxes. What is treated as a decision is also a decision. Which means that once a decision is made, it's only a potential decision, a decision candidate. If the candidate decision is followed by a decision not to treat the candidate as a decision, then it doesn't fulfil that potential. But even if there is no such subsequent decision, the actualization of a taken decision is not guaranteed. Only when there is a new decision, which uses an older one as its premise, then it effectively produces it backwards. For example, there is a decision to stop a failing project made at a project steering board meeting. But if after such a "decision" is made, a change request is issued to the contractor, then the decision made is not treated as such. Only when a certain action to start closing the project is performed, the decision to carry out that action retrospectively produces the decision to stop the project by using it as its premise.

A decision is only a decision if there is a subsequent decision to treat it as a decision.

Productive

Why *productive* paradoxes? The first reason is already obvious. Looking at organizations through a POP lens, we see that they are constantly produced by new paradoxical decisions referring to previous internal decisions and enabling following decisions. There are many other things that we associate with organizations, but what keeps them viable, as social species, is the constant production of decisions.

Decisions connect to other internal decisions, and in this way, form a closed network that creates a boundary between organizations and their environment. This is on top of the fact that the organizational membership is also subject to decisions.

Of course, organizations communicate with other organizations. And internal decisions also use external decisions as their premise, but only indirectly. Whatever is communicated from outside can only enter the internal network of communication if it is interpreted on the basis of internal references. As such, an external communication can influence an organization only if it is encoded in the internal code, the one which makes the organization what it is. In other words, communications between organizations will unavoidably be misunderstood. But this misunderstanding can be, and often is, productive. We'll explore this in more detail soon.

And last, the understanding of organizational paradoxes can be productive, which we'll show with the following practical applications.

Managing constraints

When improving a process, practice, product, or service, organizations have various approaches to gather ideas. What I have noticed at design and innovation workshops, is that people tend to censor themselves and mainly give suggestions they find realistic. Some even take pride in staying firmly on the ground, and not in the clouds, when proposing something. Another extreme, facilitated by some workshop techniques, is to fully relax all constraints and give as wild ideas as possible. There is, however, a middle way.

I have found that wearing POP glasses helps to rethink the nature of constraints that are applied before giving an idea. Constraints can be looked at as molecules made up of two types of atoms. One type is the "natural" limitations. Natural limitations can be external, such as applicable legislation, or can be internal, such as the organizational maturity level. Decision-based limitations are only internal. There is an established organizational structure, procedures, and rules, and all of them are based on decisions, which are based on decisions.

Once the constraint molecule is deconstructed into natural and decision-based limitations, it is very productive to completely release the decision-based atoms for the period of design sessions. Later, when implementation is discussed, most, but not all, of the decision-based constraints are brought back. It often turns out that some constraints can be removed more easily than previously thought. Analyzing the network of decisions also shows that some paths trace back to decisions made in the past that were relevant in circumstances which are no longer present.

Decision patterns

Making a decision is choosing between nominated options. How does this nomination happen? In most situations, there are various options that can be considered, which means that the act of nominating is also a decision, making it possible for the decision in focus to be made. If there is a way to imagine all options, then, of course, a lot of them are not considered simply due to lack of time, knowledge, or experience. The set of alternatives is further reduced by various constraints, as discussed in the previous section. What remains are two groups: feasible but rejected options and nominated options. A decision is made when one of the nominated options is selected. Once this decision is communicated, future decisions can refer to it, reject it, or ignore it. Other possibilities are also opened up, such as actions, criticism, regret, and blame, but we'll now focus on the decision topology.

If the decision is rejected or ignored, it just disappears as organizational noise. But if it is referred to by at least one subsequent decision, which is itself confirmed afterwards, then it becomes part of the decision network and takes part in the continuous self-production of the organization. And this happens every time a new decision is made. One way or another, each subsequent decision refers to at least one previous decision, and makes a choice between the remaining alternatives after other options are excluded due to constraints or preference.

Past decisions tend to be quickly forgotten. Even when they are carefully documented, new decisions attract more attention. Think of a chain of decisions where the last decision, D, refers back to decision C. C refers to B, which in turn refers to A. If decision D only refers indirectly to the first decision, A, through the chain, and D doesn't refer to A directly, then A is likely to be forgotten (later B may be forgotten too as the chain grows). This is even more likely if

A is part of a decision package, such as a plan or a strategic document.

This organizational forgetting plays an important role in the continuous self-production of organizations. It also influences the quality of decisions. Along the chain of decisions we started to follow, decision F is likely to be taken on options reduced by constraints created by decision A. Subsequently decision M will also be taken excluding better options, which were made impossible to select due to decision F.

To improve this situation, putting on POP glasses is necessary but not sufficient. What is needed is some way of recording how decisions are connected in time, their options and constraints when taken, and the relationships between decision constraints and past decisions. There are various technology options to make this easy and efficient, but they are not going to be discussed here. Nor will we explore the analytical benefits that such practices could bring. What is important is the patterns that emerge and what we can learn from them. Working with these patterns helps to develop sensitivity to the nature of decisions.

Certain types of decisions, apart from the possibilities they open and close right after they are taken, can open up more possibilities in the future or can appear as constraints for future decisions. The sensitivity for decisions patterns helps in recognizing that options like A and F are likely to constrain future decisions and have to be avoided. If you have such a habit, you may start to make decisions that do not look like the best choice of the alternatives available, but can give you more options (higher variety, as shown in Stimuli and Responses). The future is unknown, so a position with more options, like the higher diversity of the B cells, will increase your chances to deal successfully with whatever happens.

Understanding power

Power relationships exist in every organization. Using POP glasses is not your main tool for studying them, but they can be helpful for understanding power as a factor in decision-making. The power-holder often influences the nomination of options and sometimes also the decision itself, without replacing the actual decision-maker.

The influence on nominated options is realized as a reduction, as a shift, or a combination of shift and reduction. When it is a reduction, the decision-maker subject to power has to choose from fewer options than would have been at their disposal otherwise. When it is a shift, then the number of options is the same, but it's composed of different elements. The new selection is made by re-evaluating some of the excluded alternatives. The re-evaluation is caused by the power-holder banning some of the otherwise preferred options. The third case, where the options are reduced and include an otherwise excluded option, is the most frequent. All three, of course, limit autonomy and the consequences of that have been analyzed in the first chapter.

Power does not only constrain, but it also enables decision-making. If at the moment of decision-making, the options are limited by the influence of the power-holder, it was only due to a previous decision that the current decision-maker is allowed to make organizational decisions in the first place. And that previous decision, which was to hire, promote, or increase the powers of the decision-maker, was made by a person who had the power to do so, often the same current power-holder.

But it is not only people who have power. The network of connected decisions reproducing the organization has a mind of its own and also a power of its own. The power relationships change, while the decision network goes on and is always powerful. What it can also do is allow positions with lower formal authority to have higher power to influence investments and structural changes. One such case can be seen when it isn't individual decisions that are connected, but decision packages.

Decision packages

Some decisions are isolated; others come together in a package. For example, plans are packages of decisions on what is to be done, when, and by whom. Others, legal documents, for example, are packages of rules. Plans and legal documents are open for modification so that their decisions can be openly rejected while respecting their internal dependencies, but there are other kinds of decision packages which form a network of their own and obscure traceability and rejection.

In big public sector organizations, some decision packages are used to silently reject previous decisions, not by referring to the decisions individually, but to the decision package they are part of. I have closely observed a few cases that had long-lasting negative consequences in terms of millions of euros spent in vain, and that caused big delays to much-needed transformations. What typically happened was that after consulting a good number of involved parties and experts, a carefully crafted strategy was introduced and then the coordination for the implementation of that strategy was assigned to one department. That department produced an implementation plan, which fully referred to the strategy. However, a careful analysis would have shown that some of the concrete actions could be traced to concrete decisions encoded in the strategy, others not. By seemingly referring to the whole decision package, but in reality, to only some of the decisions, the plan led in an entirely different direction. Nobody in power noticed that. As the implementation plan was more recent and more concrete, it attracted more attention. This way, although it encoded decisions taken from a lower formal authority, it had the power to move the following actions in a direction that was very different from the one pointed to by the strategy.

Hidden dependencies

It's time now to see how the Ferenc's working day ended.

Ferenc's evening

Ferenc had a very productive two hours, despite the fatigue from the day. He saw no choice but to cancel his evening plans and stay late to finish all his tasks. After six, there was nobody in the open space office. It was finally quiet. He was able to focus, and by around eight, he was already ahead with the last task, the evaluation report. Ferenc had done the evaluation last week, and now he only had to compile his notes.

The report had been requested by IT auditors investigating a failed software project that had resulted in a loss of tens of millions. Ferenc did his analysis based on his specific technical expertise as specified in the request. However, he got curious beyond that and started reading the project's documentation, including the minutes of meetings, the business case, and various reports.

All his analysis was based on the work during the project, but now he became interested in what led to such a project being started in the first place. So he decided to plot the chains of decisions backwards. He did that by asking why something was decided and then looking into the project documentation for answers. Once the answer was found, he put a dot in a diagram, where the horizontal axis showed the time and the vertical axis represented power, which was estimated by the authority of the decision-maker.

The decision to start the project was based on the project plan approved by the high-level IT Board. This gave the highest dot on the plot. That approval itself was based on the evaluation of an IT Investment team, which approved the business case. The choice of the software to implement was justified previously and documented in the business case, where a Strengths, Weaknesses, Opportunities, and Threats (SWOT) analysis was carried out to compare all the nominated options. Ferenc was puzzled to see which options had been put forward. He started wondering why an obvious and quite promising alternative was not included at all.

Anyway, one of the decision premises was an IT governance principle to favour implementing off-the-shelf software over internal development. The principle was known as "Prefer Buy Over Build" and was well established and supported by the common wisdom: "Why reinvent the wheel?" Ferenc knew all too well the fallacy of "Prefer Buy Over Build". He also knew how widely shared that fallacy was, so there was no reason to look further into the past for its decision premises.

While this principle, together with other arguments, explained the exclusion of the custom development options, it did not explain why that particular software package was selected. This decision was based on a report from an influential market research company putting the vendor on top of the leaders quadrant. Of course, such justification was itself based both on the established trust in such reports and on the decision-making culture in that organization. Ferenc was very familiar with this kind of culture. Most big organizations, such as banks, telecoms, utilities, and especially public sector organizations, provide stability, which is a gravitational force for risk-averse people. The responsibility for making investment decisions is avoided using outsourcing by referring to an external authority, such as a consulting company or a market research company.

But then, Ferenc thought, even that combination of justification, the "Prefer Buy Over Build", and vendor rating report, could have been avoided if it was not for the SWOT technique. SWOT was established as a way of evaluating realization options in the guidelines for drafting business case documents. For Ferenc, as for many others, it was quite obvious that almost every SWOT can be tweaked to produce "justification" for taking a decision which had already been taken before starting to work on the SWOT. And yet, it was an unquestioned practice.

If Ferenc wasn't tired, he could have traced that thread of decisions as well. Deciding to include SWOT in the methodology for business cases was probably based on a decision of some management consultant, whose hiring was decided by some manager, who was given such powers (another decision in the topology) by somebody up the hierarchy.

It was too late now. It was time to go home.

Tracing the topology of decisions can be insightful. Yet it can also be misleading. When a car is not working, diagnosing leads to the root problem. Once the problem is fixed, the car will work again. We tend to transfer this expectation to organizations. When analyzing certain problematic situations in organizations, we again search for a root cause. And it may look like one could be found, and it is convincing on a diagram, but the reality is messier. Even when some important choices have been revealed and there is reasonable certainty that they had a major contribution to the current problematic situation, that doesn't teach us how to minimize such situations in the future.

Using the POP glasses can help with that. They reveal something which the decision threads are hiding. Ferenc's analysis linked the approval of the business case to three decisions taken previously. The first one was the use of SWOT analysis, the second was the principle of "Prefer Buy Over Build", and the third was the decision to rely on reports from a market research company when choosing software vendors. However, the actual dependencies are hidden.

They cannot be traced directly along the decision threads. The reason to select such previous decisions as decision premises was based on them being visible and stable decision premises. What made them such were various other decisions which have created them as decision premises by simply referring to them. Those confirming decisions were taken much earlier than the decision by the IT Investment team to approve the business case. And as far as looking for causes is concerned, those confirming decisions which can't be traced back logically following "why" questions, determined that particular decision allowing a project which was bound to fail.

External interactions

All the examples so far have shown how POP glasses can be used to understand phenomena within organizations. POP glasses can also be used to better understand what goes on between organizations.

Some small organizations interact more with individual clients and less with other organizations. Yet, they can't avoid interacting with organizations. All government authorities and most of their vendors are organizations. With bigger organizations and with those having business-to-business transactions, the majority of interactions with their environment are interactions with other organizations.

Seen through POP lenses, organizations are what they are and continue to exist due to their closed network of communications and more particularly decisions. Organizations make offers, place orders, and deliver goods and services to each other. They interact in various ways. But the results of these interactions depend on their internal structure and organizational culture more than on the nature of the interactions.

If one organization communicates with another, the

communication is taken up by the second organization only in reference to its internal network of communications. For people from both organizations, this communication may have the same meaning, but the closed internal network of communication and decisions can only accept it based on its own interpretation.

More than once I've seen this manifested in the way projects were evaluated by different stakeholders. For example, a project which had met its objectives, somehow still did not satisfy the client and was perceived as a failure. And other projects, which were over time and budget, or delivered a smaller scope than agreed, were remembered as successful. The evaluation also changed in time. Some projects, rated as successful at their time of completion, were seen as failures a year after and vice versa.

With POP glasses on, we can see that communications, such as requirements and objectives, even when agreed and documented, mean one thing for the vendor organization and another for the client organization. This points to a new balance, the balance between success and satisfaction. It's logical to expect a successful project based on agreed criteria to lead to client satisfaction, but it is not necessarily the case. And while I thought that this is true mainly in software projects, it turned out it isn't related to that specific domain. There were, for example, construction projects using the same project methodology and project manager that clearly showed duality between success and satisfaction. One of them delivered more than the initially agreed scope, within deadline and budget, but the client was dissatisfied. The other project was actually over time and over budget, yet the client was happy.

It seems that aiming only to meet the measurable criteria for success doesn't guarantee satisfaction, which itself cannot be measured but is assumed to follow, based on the criteria for success. Success and satisfaction influence each other, but in a dynamic way, which needs attention throughout the project. They are yet another complex organizational balance.

Summary

Decisions in organizations are paradoxical, yet productive. They are paradoxical because at the same time, they communicate their alternative and that they are not their alternative. They are also paradoxical because they are produced backwards by the decisions that they enable.

Organizational decisions refer to each other and form a closed network. This network produces the organization and makes it distinct from its environment.

Understanding organizations as something produced by a closed network of decisions can be productive. For example, lifting decision-based constraints when improving processes and services allows more variety of ideas and possibilities to overcome some of the decision-based constraints.

Analyzing decision topologies brings insights into how to improve decision-making. That practice can also create the habit of seeing decision patterns when evaluating options. Such habits help in avoiding options which look attractive at the moment but might seriously constrain future decision options.

Power relations can be seen as the power-holder reducing and shifting the options of the decision-maker, who is the power subject.

Sometimes decisions come combined in decision packages, such as plans and strategies. These packages refer to each other in a way that some of the older decisions are confirmed, others are ignored, while seemingly the whole package was respected. This can lead to good quality decisions being replaced by bad quality decisions during execution.

There are hidden dependencies between decisions that cannot

be traced directly along the decision path. A decision path can lead back to some visible past decision that can be seen as a root cause. But that decision was made selectable by other decisions which are the actual conditions leading to the current situation.

When organizations interact, such interaction is confused as communication. What interactions actually do is to trigger changes in the other organization, but they are interpreted according to the internal logic of that organization. This is why when a client commissions a project, neither the clarity of the requirements, nor the agreement on success criteria can guarantee client satisfaction. Success and satisfaction are not tightly linked and influence each other in complex ways.

These are only a few examples of new insights coming from wearing POP glasses. Try them on, and you'll find other ways they can be helpful. The POP glasses might not be as easy to wear as the previous four pairs, but they might work where others don't, and they may bring a new perspective when used in combination.

NOTES

1. Do you know, for example, that you can base most of mathematics not on numbers but only on the concept of boundary?

The boundary algebra was developed between 1991 and 1993 by William Bricken and Jeffrey James (Bricken, 2019).

2. We need to map things to symbols they stand for.

This mapping is known as a "triangle of reference" or "semiotic triangle" where a *symbol* stands for an *object* which we can understand because it symbolises a *thought* that refers to the same object (Ogden & Richards, 1923).

3. It is much more natural to see adding as putting things together.

The choice of an abstract word over a natural equivalent for the same action supported the development of symbolic thinking in mathematics which was enabling but – and there is little awareness about that – was also constraining (Bricken, 2019). If the position about the constraining role is controversial, in terms of education it is less so. Many children hate mathematics in school because of the need to constantly do abstract mapping to symbols which has no correspondence to their daily experience. This is also due to the choice of words for arithmetic operations. In English, borrowing from Latin, adding (from *addire,* to give towards) and subtracting (from *subtrahere,* to pull away) replaced the natural putting things together, assembling, and respectively taking out or pulling away. If you have | | | candies in your pocket and you take away | |, there will be | left. When expressing this in mathematics, you have to not only use symbols but also abstract words. Understanding 3 - 2 = 1 does not only require constant mapping, but also "-" is mapped to "subtract" and not to "take away". In some languages this split was not made. In Bulgarian, for example, to say you *take out* 2 candies from your pocket, you'd use the verb *изваждам,* which is the same word a mathematician, a school teacher, or university professor would use for *subtract.*

4. Unlike stones, organisms and organizations create their boundaries themselves.

The technical term for this phenomenon is "self-individuation".

> *Organisms actively and continuously produce a distinction between themselves and their environment where none existed before they appeared and where none will remain after they are gone.* (Di Paolo, Cuffari, & De Jaegher, 2018)

5. What makes it alive is that it produces itself every moment.

According to the theory of autopoiesis of Maturana and Varela, living systems are organized as a closed network of mutually enabling processes (Maturana & Varela, 1980). Later Varela more formally defined the necessary and sufficient conditions for a system to be autopoietic (Varela, 2000):

(a) it has a semipermeable boundary,

(b) the boundary is produced from within the system, and

(c) it encompasses reactions that regenerate the components of the system.

Against such a test, amoebas are autopoietic, but mitochondria are not, for they don't satisfy the third condition, and neither are viruses for they satisfy neither the second nor the third condition (Thompson, 2010).

For a detailed overview of applications of autopoiesis in domains outside biology, such as in organizations and other social systems, see *Self-Producing Systems - Implications and Applications of Autopoiesis* (Mingers, 1995).

6. The immune system, for example, is able to make a boundary by creating a closed network of cells.

Francisco Varela showed how not only cells but also other systems, such as the metabolic, nervous, and immune systems are autopoietic. The way the latter works is described in Varela and Coutinho (1991). For a short summary, see note 6 after the "Stability and Diversity" chapter.

7. A message can be uttered, can be understood, and still not represent information.

Communication, according to Luhmann, is the unity of distinction between utterance, information, and understanding. Understanding is the distinction between utterance and information (Seidl, Becker, & Luhmann, 2005). Yet, something can be understood without being information.

> *An item of information has to be new, it has to be surprising (however minimally), and therefore always relates to the state of knowledge of the system. This distinguishes between meaning and information. Meaning stays the same even when repeated, and repetition is only to be recognized as repetition if this is so. When information is repeated, by contrast, it loses its informational value.* (Luhmann, 2018)

That's why I put meaning as the second component of communication and information as the third.

8. But that message wouldn't carry information to him, as he already knows about the meeting at two.

When a message is repeated it loses its informational value. The logic of this can be seen in the first law of form (Spencer-Brown, 1972): "The value of a call made again is the value of the call". In other words, to re-call is to call. The following three examples should make this clearer. If you draw a circle and name it X, the X does not add meaning. The circle stands for itself and the X stands for the circle. If you highlight something and then underline it, that's just another way of highlighting unless you assign a specific meaning. But in that case, it will be drawing another distinction. If you go to the ice cream shop, you may say "vanilla" or point to the container of vanilla ice cream. Both ways signal the same request. To re-call is to call.

So when a message is repeated, it keeps its meaning value, but it loses its information value.

9. He is already *in*formed.

This implies a change of state, a change of the form. But nicely, *in*formed also suggests that the change is made from within. That's not only with information, but with every action that makes a change. If you kick a stone, the movement of the stone will depend on your kick. If you kick a dog, the reaction of the dog will depend on the dog. If you write something on a piece of paper, the change of the paper is from without, but if you tell the same information to somebody, her change is from within. In a way, there is no transmission of information through language:

> *So long as language is considered to be denotative it will be necessary to look at it as a means for the transmission of information, as if something were transmitted from organism to organism, in a manner such that the domain of uncertainties of the 'receiver' should be reduced according to the specifications of the 'sender'. However, when it is recognized that language is connotative and not denotative, and that its function is to orient the orientee within his cognitive domain without regard for the cognitive domain of the orienter, it becomes apparent that there is no transmission of information through language. It behooves the orientee, as a result of an independent internal operation upon his own state, to choose where to orient his cognitive domain; the choice is caused by the 'message', but the orientation thus produced is independent of what the 'message' represents for the oriented.* (Maturana & Varela, 1980)

For a recent further development of this idea, see *From participatory sense-making to language: There and back again* (Cuffari, Ezequiel, & De Jaegher, 2014) and *Linguistic bodies: The continuity between life and language* (Di Paolo, Cuffari, & De Jaegher, 2018).

10. Information is what makes the difference.

To be able to perceive something, it should be distinguished from what it is not. But this can be just noise, which we can distinguish from silence. Not every difference is information. Information is only that "difference which makes a difference" (Bateson, 1972).

Evan Thompson, building on Bateson and Susan Oyama, suggested the following definition: "Information, dynamically conceived, is the making of a difference that makes a difference for some-*body* somewhere" (Thompson, 2010, emphasis in the original), adding the important aspects of co-creation, embodiment, and environment.

11. When Ferenc decided what to wear that day, that's not a decision which participates in the organization he works for.

That holds even in extreme cases, like Ferenc deciding to show up in the office wearing full scuba gear. It is a similar case to the one about external interactions, the last section of the chapter. Ferenc, and any other person working for an organization, is not part of that organization but is structurally coupled with it. And a strange personal decision like showing up with full scuba gear can trigger organizational decisions, but what this will cause will be determined by the closed network of organizational decisions, and not by an affecting decision of a system structurally coupled with it.

12. "Only *those* questions which are in principle undecidable, *we* can decide."

Decidable questions depend on a chosen convention, and the rest on the one who decides. There are numerous inventions to present the latter as the former in order to avoid responsibility (von Foerster, 2003):

> *Objectivity, Pontius Pilate, hierarchies, and other devices are all derivations of a choice between a pair of in principle undecidable questions which are, "Am I apart from the universe?" Meaning whenever I look, I'm looking as if through a peephole upon an unfolding universe; or, "Am I part of the universe?" Meaning whenever I act, I'm changing myself and the universe as well.* (ibid.)

13. It could be generally accepted conventions (axioms, for example), or more specific conventions, such as the banks' "Rule of 78".

The Rule of 78 is a method used by some lenders to calculate interest charges on a loan. The interest on a one-year loan is divided into portions so that 12 portions are paid the first month, 11 in the second and so on until the last month only one portion is paid. The sum of all portions with such a distribution is 78 where the name of the rule comes from. Such a rule is applied for loans repaid over a longer period but keeps its name, although then the number of portions of interest is bigger than 78.

14. [W]here a SWOT analysis was carried out to compare all the nominated options.

SWOT is an abbreviation of strengths, weaknesses, opportunities, and threats. It's a planning technique where a proposal or a business situation and outlook are evaluated comparing internal strong and weak points, and the relevant opportunities and threats from the environment. In spite of its weaknesses, maybe due to its simplicity, this technique is still widely used in strategic and project evaluation and planning.

15. Ferenc knew all too well the fallacy of "Prefer Buy Over Build".

For a detailed description of that popular delusion, see *Fallacy #2 "It will cost more to re-invent the wheel"* in *Software Wasteland* (McComb, 2018).

16. There were, for example, construction projects using the same project methodology and project manager that clearly showed duality between success and satisfaction.

Usher and Whitty reported two project cases (Usher & Whitty, 2017). The first one was a good project when measured by the standard indicators for being delivered within time and budget and the required quality, but it left the client unsatisfied. The second project was over budget and planned duration, but produced the opposite effect. Both projects were in the same industry, with the same project manager and methodology. The authors explain the paradox by the two sides of the project belonging to different organizations, which functioned as closed self-referential systems, having their own internal codes.

EPILOGUE

ORGANIZING IS a balancing act of balancing acts. There are three kinds of acts that are essential. They are closely connected, yet different. Organizations work well when they are able to maintain all three essential balances at all scales of organizational identity. As there are infinite ways to maintain them, this book offers no recipes. Instead, it provides metaphorical glasses and goes on a journey to see how different organisms and organizations keep the balances. Apart from the three essential balances, there is one more pair of glasses for a meta-balance, and another for organizational paradoxes.

The aim of the book is to help develop new thinking habits. In view of this, you will probably identify with one of the following two groups.

First, you already had these thinking habits before reading the book. Then I hope the book strengthened them and enriched the way you think about organizations.

Second, if you didn't have these thinking habits, but you found the arguments convincing, reading the book probably planted the seeds. If that's the case, and you want to grow them, the first thing to do is to read the book once again, and after that, you may consider the following tips (yes, finally some advice).

Throughout the book, you saw the balances appearing in different types of organisms, organizations, and situations. Noticing these patterns is a skill that takes time to develop. The patterns show that some things are invariant, and yet they have their contexts and their nuances. Noticing the patterns of balances in new situations confirms and exploits the value of the skill, while the knowledge about the different contexts and nuances enhances the applicability and usefulness of the skill.

But how can you train and enhance that skill?

The focus of the book is on how the balances play out in what we call organizations, yet the balances are more widely spread, and appear in everything that has internally maintained or emergent organization. The last condition – to be internally maintained or emergent – is important. A software application has organization, but it is created and maintained by a software engineer, not by the application itself. You won't find the balances there. But when a user interacts with the application, new properties emerge from that dynamic interaction, and now all four balances are there. Being aware of such situations will help you learn from them.

And apart from similar particular situations, you will always find the balances at the scales below organization (personal) and above organization (society).

Working with the balances at the personal level is an easy and affordable workout because we have ourselves handy at all times. There are many useful practice areas at the personal level, but you can start with these two: sports and routines.

For sports, I'll use tennis as an example. The first step is just to observe and experience balances.

The quality of a shot depends greatly on the right distance between body and ball. When hitting the ball, if you are too close or too far from it, you can bet it will be a bad shot. That balance is very important. Achieving it is easier when the ball comes close to you, but very difficult when you have to run to reach the ball. Knowing in advance when to stop the sprint is impossible. What you do at the end of the run is to take small adjusting steps. Remember the small adaptations from Chapter 1, "Autonomy and Cohesion"? That's the role of these adjusting steps. And a big adaptation is, of course, learning to play better. There are also situational adaptations where during a match you learn the particular style and strategy of the opponent and you adapt to it. As already discussed, the difficulty is that you must adapt to somebody who is adapting to your adaptations to their adaptations, and so on.

Apart from the body–ball balance, it's important how the non-dominant hand is balancing the dominant, and how well your body is balanced. The latter is difficult to detect because – presuming you play sober – you rarely lose balance. But the way you keep it is what matters, and that's not easy to sense because you are not conscious of it. To diagnose it, you need to do something unusual. For example, when you finish the shot, if you stay for a few extra moments with your racket at the final position, you may find that you need an extra step to keep your balance. That's how you discover that you have to work on it.

Once you are well aware of all the specific balances, you can start putting on the different pairs of glasses from the book.

When you serve, the ball should land in the service box. That rule, together with the lines drawn on the court, provides cohesion. But you have autonomy as to how you hit the ball (flat, slice, or spin) and where in the service box to place it. Imagine this balance is broken. The area of service box is now not the established 283.5 square feet (26.3 m^2), but is very small, say only 10 square feet (0.93 m^2). This makes it incredibly difficult for you to hit a successful serve, and very easy for your opponent to return it because she'll always wait for the ball in the right place. As a result, this version of tennis is predictable and boring and will quickly die.

You need stability in your game, otherwise there will be many unforced errors. To get a stable backhand, you need to practise a lot of backhands. But if you only practise that, then your forehand, serve, volley, and smash will be unstable. That's why you need a diversity of skills to be successful.

During a match, you should exploit your strengths, but that can only be successful if you keep exploring your opponent's weaknesses.

Overall, this adds up to the fact, more obvious in sport than in other situations, that in order to have a chance of winning, the variety of your responses must at least equal the variety of your opponent's stimuli. That variety comes from speed, agility, and stamina as well as from the different shots you can use, the styles of play you can master, the speed of your decision-making, and your ability to read and perhaps anticipate the play.

This was for tennis, but you can figure it out for your sport. Importantly you should experience it. Watching your favourite sport may also be useful, but it is not nearly as effective as doing it yourself.

The second opportunity area for honing your observational skills at a personal level are routines. The story about Emma's morning from Chapter 4, "Stimuli and Responses", was an example of that. The ten small events, which illustrated the different manifestations of the Stimuli–Responses balance, happen to many people at the beginning of a working day. This and other routines are full of opportunities to observe interesting phenomena. And there is a bonus: looking at them with the new pairs of glasses will make them less boring.

The level above organizations – that of society – is also a good place to develop the new thinking habits. Some balances are easier to see there because they are amplified through the observations of the media (both traditional and social), politics, and science. For example, the Covid-19 pandemic made very clear – among other things – the shift in the balance of autonomy and cohesion at the national and international level. Normally centralization is not a good way to achieve cohesion, but in times of crisis, the cohesion created through centralization seems acceptable. In a crisis, people are more willing to forgo certain freedoms to get more protection. Where that willingness reaches its limits, say tracing movements and contacts, is the stretch of the current shift of the balance.

Other sources of insight into balances, and ones which were heavily exploited in the book, are the endless examples from biology, the evolution of species, and the various ways to deal with challenges and uncertainty for which we have historical records.

Don't forget to use the glasses in combination, and not only for the balances, but remember all five pairs. For example, you may have noticed the following paradox: people striving for diversity usually don't tolerate diversity of opinions about diversity.

The skills of seeing, restoring, and maintaining balances should be applied to themselves.

The skill of seeing the patterns this book talks about should be balanced with an ability to consciously ignore them. Seeing the patterns should not prevent you from being conscious of when something different and more important is going on.

In parallel with being more observant for patterns of the balances, it's important to train the skill of zooming in and out. To be able to quickly go from the forest to a tree, to a branch, and to a branch of a branch, and back. And that's still not enough, because this is only above the ground. There is a lot going on below the soil in the wood wide web of fungi connecting the roots. And again, the skill to quickly zoom in and out, and to pan above and below the ground, should be balanced with the skill to stay focused.

Observing and zooming needs to be applied in practice, so I'll end with a few words about transferring the lessons from one example to your situation. This is the most difficult balancing act. How do we learn from these observations without expecting the magic that working with computers makes us expect – the magic of copy/paste and drag and drop? And that awareness is applicable not only when transferring experience or observation from another area, but even within the domain of organizations. A direct transfer will never work because of the different context and time. But even if you try to do the same thing in the same context and almost at the same time, it may not work. What's more, it may produce an effect of a different magnitude. For example, making a cut in a loose fishing net will have only a local effect, while the same cut in the same place when the net is stretched will spread the damage throughout the net. And a fishing net – as well as any organization – can change its state from loose to taut very quickly.

Using the glasses to see the balances is also a balancing act. You have the autonomy in when and how to use them, but the framework provides guidance and through it, cohesion. You can benefit from the routine of using the glasses, but you should have a diverse set, bigger than the essential ones provided here. Exploiting these glasses will help to diagnose and design organizations, but you should keep exploring new ways.

Life is changing. Now faster than ever. New business models will replace the current ones. There will be new methodologies and new management fads. Maybe hierarchy will go or be dynamically switched on and off when needed. Maybe organizations as we know them will disappear and completely different structures will replace them. But one thing is certain: as long as there is life, the need for organizing will remain, and the balances you read about in this book will still hold and still be essential.

ACKNOWLEDGMENTS

I've been lucky to get so much support and valuable feedback.

I'm grateful to Lars Sudmann, who encouraged me to start writing this book, the main ideas of which were previously only provided through workshops. I delivered the first workshop in 2014 in Athens after an invitation from Nicos Kourounakis, whom I want to thank not only for that, but also for convincing me to look for a way to mould these ideas – communicated in a different way up to then – for a broader audience.

My writing process resembled Agile software development. I made a prototype – the first chapter – and shared it for "testing". Then I used the feedback not only to improve it but to guide the writing of the next chapters. I did that for a few more iterations and continued to trim my sails. Yet the biggest changes in terms of form and style were decided on the basis of the reviews of that first prototype. And so I'd like to thank all who were brave enough to read it and so kind to share their thoughts on it: Benjamin P. Taylor, Steve Morlidge, Jonathan Huxley, Wendy Christiaens, Richard Dijkstra, Mark Lambertz, Olivier Risack, Eddy Vanderlinden, Bart Du Bois, Jean Vercruysse, Maria Podlasek-Ziegler, Maciej

Krzysztofowicz, Nicos Kourounakis, Wilson Mvula, and Nancy Swinkels.

The feedback from my wife, Sylvia, was sometimes difficult to take and act upon. But it was especially valuable coming from somebody with a bunch of published books and at the same time outside the topic bubble.

I'm grateful to Luc Hoebeke, for what I learned from him, through his writings and directly from our discussions, and for writing the foreword to this book.

Last and most, I want to thank my editor, Rob Worth, for his excellent work and collaboration.

REFERENCES

Allin, E. F. (1975). Evolution of the mammalian middle ear. *Journal of Morphology*.

Ashby, W. R. (1960). *Design for a brain: The origin of adaptive behaviour.* Springer.

Ashby, W. R. (2015 [1956]). *An introduction to cybernetics.* Martino Fine Books.

Aulin-Ahmavaara, A. Y. (1979). The Law of Requisite Hierarchy. *Kybernetes*.

Baecker, D. (2006). The Form of the Firm. *Organization: The Critical Journal on Organization, Theory and Society*.

Barandiaran, X. E., & Di Paolo, E. A. (2014). A genealogical map of the concept of habit. *Frontiers in Human Neuroscience*.

Barrett, F. J. (1998). Coda—Creativity and Improvisation in Jazz and Organizations: Implications for Organizational Learning. *Organization Science*.

Bateson, G. (1972). Form, Substance, and Difference. In G. Bateson, *Steps to an Ecology of Mind: Collected Essays in*

Anthropology, Psychiatry, Evolution, and Epistemology. Jason Aronson Inc.

Beer, S. (1975). *Platform for change.* John Wiley & Sons.

Beer, S. (1980). *The heart of enterprise.* Wiley.

Beer, S. (1993). *Designing freedom (CBC Massey Lectures).* House of Anansi Press.

Bernhard, P. (2013). *The certainty of uncertainty: Dialogues introducing constructivism.* Imprint Academic.

Boisot, M., & McKelvey, B. (2011). Complexity and Organization–Environment Relations: Revisiting Ashby's Law of Requisite Variety. In P. Allen, S. Maguire, & B. McKelvey, *The SAGE Handbook of Complexity and Management.* SAGE Publications Ltd.

Bricken, W. (2019). *Iconic arithmetic volume I: The design of mathematics for human understanding.* Unary Press.

Brunsson, N. (1985). *The irrational organization: Irrationality as a basis for organizational action and change.* Wiley.

Brunsson, N. (2006). *Mechanisms of hope.* Copenhagen Business School Press.

Brunsson, N. (2007). *The consequences of decision-making.* Oxford University Press.

Brunsson, N. (2009). *Reform as routine: Organizational change and stability in the modern world.* Oxford University Press.

Brush, S. B., Taylor, J. E., & Bellon, M. R. (1992). Technology adoption and biological diversity in Andean potato agriculture. *Journal of Development Economics.*

Buhrmann, T., Di Paolo, E. A., & Barandiaran, X. (2013). A dynamical systems account of sensorimotor contingencies. *Frontiers in Psychology.*

Burns, J. G., & Dyer, A. G. (2008). Diversity of speed-accuracy strategies benefits social insects. *Current Biology.*

Cárdenas, J. P., Vidal, G., Urbina, C., Olivares, G., & Fuentes,

M. A. (2018). Social crises. A network model approach. *Physica A.*

Campbell, D. B. (2006). *Besieged: Siege warfare in the ancient world.* Osprey Publishing.

Centola, D., & Baronchelli, A. (2015). The spontaneous emergence of conventions: An experimental study of cultural evolution. *Proceedings of the National Academy of Sciences.*

Colombetti, G. (2014). *The feeling body: Affective science meets the enactive mind.* The MIT Press.

Cook, Z., Franks, D. W., & Robinson, E. J. (2013). Exploration versus exploitation in polydomous ant colonies. *Journal of Theoretical Biology.*

Cooper, M. D. (2015). The early history of B cells. *Nature Reviews Immunology.*

Crisp, C. B., & Jarvenpaa, S. L. (2013). Swift trust in global virtual teams: Trusting beliefs and normative actions. *Journal of Personnel Psychology.*

Cuffari, E. C., Ezequiel, P. D., & Hanne, J. D. (2014). From participatory sense-making to language: there and back again. *Phenomenology and the Cognitive Sciences.*

Del Gandio, J. (2012, June 28). *Freedom vs. Autonomy: A tale of two logics.* Retrieved from Philosophers for Change: https://philosophersforchange.org/2012/06/28/freedom-vs-autonomy-a-tale-of-two-logics/

Deming, W. E. (2000). *Out of the crisis.* The MIT Press.

Di Paolo, E. A., Cuffari, E. C., & De Jaegher, H. (2018). *Linguistic bodies: The continuity between life and language.* The MIT Press.

Diamantopoulou, S., & Christidou, D. (2019). Museum encounters: A choreography of visitors' bodies in interaction. *Museum Management and Curatorship.*

Diamond, J. (2012). *The world until yesterday: What can we learn from traditional societies?* Penguin Books.

Dimaggio, P. J., & Powel, W. W. (1983). The Iron Cage Revisited: Institutional Isomorphism and Collective Rationality in Organizational Fields. *American Sociological Review.*

Egbert, M., & Cañamero, L. (2014). Habit-based Regulation of Essential Variables. *Artificial Life Conference Proceedings 14.* MIT Press.

Foerster, H. v. (2003). *Understanding understanding: Essays on cybernetics and cognition.* Springer.

Foerster, H. v. (2013). *The beginning of heaven and Earth has no name: Seven days with second-order cybernetics.* Fordham University Press.

Forrester Research. (2019). *The Cost Of Losing Creativity.* Forrester Research.

Gartner. (2019, July 29). *Newsroom.* Retrieved from Gartner.com: https://www.gartner.com/en/newsroom/press-releases/2019-07-29-gartner-says-worldwide-iaas-public-cloud-services-market-grew-31point3-percent-in-2018

Gibson, C. B., & Birkinshaw, J. (2004). The Antecedents, Consequences, and Mediating Role of Organizational Ambidexterity. *The Academy of Management Journal.*

Glanville, R. (2007). Try again. Fail again. Fail better: The cybernetics in design and the design in cybernetics. *Kybernetes.*

Goland, C. (1993). Field Scattering as Agricultural Risk Management: A Case Study from Cuyo Cuyo, Department of Puno, Peru. *Mountain Research and Development.*

Goodhart, C. (1984). Problems of Monetary Management:

The U.K. Experience. In *Monetary Theory and Practice.* Palgrave.

Gould, S. J., & Vrba, E. S. (1982). Exaptation-A Missing Term in the Science of Form. *Paleobiology.*

Gray, D. (2014). *The connected company.* O'Reilly Media.

Harper, D. (2018, 04 10). Retrieved from Online Etymology Dictionary: https://www.etymonline.com/word/deal

Harrison, D. A., Price, K. H., & Florey, A. T. (2002). Time, Teams, and Task Performance: Changing Effects of Surface- and Deep-Level Diversity on Group Functioning. *Academy of Management Journal.*

Harrison, I. H. (1883). *Kriloff's original fables.* Remington & Co.

Hauge, M. (2018, 11 30). *Six-stage plot structure.* Retrieved from Story Mastery: https://www.storymastery.com/wp-content/uploads/2018/11/6-Stage-Plot-Structure-Chart-color_.pdf

Hawksworth, D. L., & Lücking, R. (2017). Chapter 4: Fungal Diversity Revisited: 2.2 to 3.8 Million Species. In *The Fungal Kingdom.*

Henri, S., Vlachou, C., & Thiran, P. (2018). Multi-Armed Bandit in Action: Optimizing Performance in Dynamic Hybrid Networks. *Transactions on Networking.*

Heylighen, F., & Joslyn, C. (2001). Cybernetics and Second-Order Cybernetics. In R. A. Meyers, *Encyclopedia of Physical Science and Technology.* New York: Academic Press.

Hoebeke, L. (1994). *Making work systems better: A practitioner's reflections.* Wiley.

Hoebeke, L. (2014). *The elephant and the lion: An enquiry into the roots of democracy.* Retrieved from http://www.simenvandergoot.nl/media/The_elephant_and_the_Lion.pdf

Hoverstadt, P. (2008). *The fractal organization: Creating sustainable organizations with the viable system model.* John Wiley & Sons.

Human, H., Nicolson, S. W., & Dietemann, V. (2006). Do honeybees, Apis mellifera scutellata, regulate humidity in their nest? *The Science of Nature.*

International Organization for Standardization. (2011, December). ISO/IEC/IEEE 42010:2011 Systems and software engineering – Architecture description.

Jonas, H. (2001). *The phenomenon of life: Toward a philosophical biology.* Northwestern University Press.

Kimberly, J. R. (1981). Managerial Innovation. In P. C. Nystrom, & W. H. Starbuck, *Handbook of Organizational Design* (pp. 84-104). Elsevier.

Klein, K. E. (2002). *The Bottom Line on Startup Failures.* Retrieved from Bloomberg: https://www.bloomberg.com/news/articles/2002-03-03/the-bottom-line-on-startup-failures

Knudsen, M. (2017). From evidence-based management to management of non-knowledge. *Emergence: Complexity and Organization.*

Kuleshov, V., & Precup, D. (2014). Algorithms for multi-armed bandit problems. *Journal of Machine Learning Research.*

Kurtz, C. F., & Snowden, D. J. (2003). The new dynamics of strategy: Sense-making in a complex and complicated world. *IBM Systems Journal.*

Laeng, B., & Teodorescu, D.-S. (2002). Eye scanpaths during visual imagery reenact those of perception of the same visual scene. *Cognitive Science.*

Lakoff, G., & Johnson, M. (2003). *Metaphors we live by.* University of Chicago Press.

Lakoff, G., & Johnson, M. (2008). *Philosophy in the flesh: The embodied mind and its challenge to western thought.* Basic Books.

Lanzara, G. F., & Morner, M. (2003). The Knowledge Ecology of Open-Source Software Projects.

Livingstone, M. (2008). *Vision and art: The biology of seeing.* Harry N. Abrams.

Lord, R. G., Dihn, J. E., & Hoffman, E. L. (2015). A Quantum Approach to Time and Organizational Change. *Academy of Management Review.*

Lu, J. G., Joel, B., Vardi, Y., & Weitz, E. (2017). The dark side of experiencing job autonomy: Unethical behavior. *Journal of Experimental Social Psychology.*

Luhmann, N. (1995). *Social systems.* Stanford University Press.

Luhmann, N. (2018). *Organization and decision.* Cambridge University Press.

Mann, R. P., & Helbing, D. (2016). Optimal incentives for collective intelligence. *PNAS.*

Mansfield, M. (2019, March 28). *STARTUP STATISTICS – The Numbers You Need to Know.* Retrieved from Small Business Trends: https://smallbiztrends.com/2019/03/startup-statistics-small-business.html

March, J. G. (1991). Exploration and Exploitation in Organizational Learning. *Organization Science.*

Maturana, H. R. (2015). What Is Sociology? *Constructivist Foundations.*

Maturana, H. R., & Varela, F. J. (1980). *Autopoiesis and cognition: The realization of the living.* D. Reidel Publishing Company.

McComb, D. (2018). *Software wasteland: How the application-centric mindset is hobbling our enterprises.* Technics Publications.

McLachlan, G. R., & Liversidge, R. (1978). *Roberts birds of*

South Africa. The Trustees of the John Voelcker Bird Book Fund.

Merali, Y., & Allen, P. (2011). Complexity and Systems Thinking. In P. Allen, S. Maguire, & B. McKelvey, *The SAGE Handbook of Complexity and Management.* SAGE Publications Ltd.

Meyerson, D., Weick, K. E., & Kramer, R. M. (1995). Swift Trust and Temporary Groups. In *Trust in Organizations: Frontiers of Theory and Research.* SAGE Publications.

Mingers, J. (1995). *Self-producing systems - Implications and applications of autopoiesis.* Springer.

Mitchell, M. (2011). *Complexity: A guided tour.* Oxford University Press.

Morlidge, S. (2017). *The little book of beyond budgeting.* Troubador Publishing Ltd.

Mullins, J., & Komisar, R. (2009). *Getting to plan B: Breaking through to a better business model.* Harvard Business Review Press.

Núñez, R. E., & Sweetser, E. (2005). Aymara, where the future is behind you: Convergent evidence from language and gesture in the crosslinguistic comparison of spatial construals of time. *Cognitive Science.*

New South Wales Government State Archives & Records. (2020, 03 15). *Sydney Opera House Guide.* Retrieved from New South Wales Governmnet State Archives & Records: https://www.records.nsw.gov.au/archives/collections-and-research/guides-and-indexes/sydney-opera-house-guide

Number of apps available in leading app stores as of 1st quarter 2020. (2020, 06 23). Retrieved from Statista.com: https://www.statista.com/statistics/276623/number-of-apps-available-in-leading-app-stores/

Ogden, C. K., & Richards, I. A. (1923). *The meaning of*

meaning: A study of the influence of language upon thought and of the science of symbolism. Harcourt.

O'Regan, J. K., & Noë, A. (2001). A sensorimotor account of vision and visual consciousness. *Behavioral and Brain Sciences.*

O'Reilly III, C. A., & Tushman, M. L. (2013). Organizational Ambidexterity: Past, Present and Future. *Academy of Management Perspectives.*

Press, W. H. (2009). Bandit solutions provide unified ethical models for randomized clinical trials and comparative effectiveness research. *PNAS.*

Price, M. (2018, 11 28). *Kill Your Personas.* Retrieved from Medium: https://medium.com/microsoft-design/kill-your-personas-1c332d4908cc

Rasche, A., & Seidl, D. (2017). A Luhmannian perspective on strategy: Strategy as paradox and meta-communication. *Critical Perspectives on Accounting.*

Rodriguez, H. P., Henke, R. M., Bibi, S., & Shortell, S. M. (2016). The Exnovation of Chronic Care Management Processes by Physician Organizations. *The Milbank Quarterly.*

Roy, M. H., & Dugal, S. S. (1998). Developing trust: The importance of cognitive flexibility and co–operative contexts. *Management Decision.*

Russo, R. (1998). *Straight man.* Vintage.

Schulz, K. (2011). *Being wrong: Adventures in the margin of error.* Ecco.

Seidl, D., Becker, K. H., & Luhmann, N. (2005). *Niklas Luhmann and organization studies.* Liber.

Sheldrake, M. (2020). *Entangled life: How fungi make our worlds, change our minds & shape our futures.* Random House.

Shen, W., Wang, J., Jiang, Y.-G., & Zha, H. (2015). Portfolio

Choices with Orthogonal Bandit Learning. *Twenty-Fourth International Joint Conference on Artificial Intelligence.*

Spencer-Brown, G. (1972). *Laws of form.* The Julian Press, Inc.

Stanley, M. (2016). Why should physicists study history? *Physics Today.*

Strathern, M. (1997). 'Improving ratings': Audit in the British University system. *European Review.*

Swings, T., Van den Bergh, B., Wuyts, S., Oeyen, E., Voordeckers, K., Verstrepen, K. J., . . . Michiels, J. (2017). Adaptive tuning of mutation rates allows fast response to lethal stress in Escherichia coli.

Taleb, N. (2018). *Skin in the game: Hidden asymmetries in daily life.* Random House.

Taylor, J. R., & Van Every , E. J. (1999). *The emergent organization: Communication as its site and surface.* Routledge.

Technology Review. (1999). Melted Chocolate to Microwave. *Technology Review.*

Thompson, E. (2010). *Mind in life.* Harvard University Press.

Torchia, M., Calabrò, A., & Morner, M. (2015). Board of Directors' Diversity, Creativity, and Cognitive Conflict. *International Studies of Management & Organization.*

Trivers, R. (2014). *Deceit and self-deception.* Penguin Books Ltd.

Tsoukas, H., & Chia, R. (2002). On Organizational Becoming: Rethinking Organizational Change. *Organization Science.*

Usher, G., & Whitty, S. J. (2017). Project Management Yinyang: Coupling project success and client satisfaction. *Project Management Research and Practice.*

Vanhaute, E., Paping, R., & Ó Gráda, C. (2006). The European subsistence crisis of 1845-1850: A comparative perspective. *XIV International Economic History Congress of the International Economic History Association.* Helsinki.

Varela, F. (2000). *El fenómeno de la vida.* Dolmen Ediciones.

Varela, F. J. (1979). *Principles of biological autonomy.* North Holland.

Varela, F. J., & Coutinho, A. (1991). Second generation immune networks. *Immunology Today.*

Varela, F. J., Thompson, E., & Rosch, E. (1992). *The embodied mind: Cognitive science and human experience.* MIT Press.

Velitchkov, I. (2015, September 27). *From Distinction to Value and Back.* Retrieved from http://www.strategicstructures.com/?p=957

Verborgh, R. (2017, 12 20). *Paradigm shifts for the decentralized Web.* Retrieved from https://ruben.verborgh.org/: https://ruben.verborgh.org/blog/2017/12/20/paradigm-shifts-for-the-decentralized-web/

von Foerster, H. (2003). Ethics and Second-Order Cybernetics. In H. von Foerster, *Understanding understanding.* Springer.

Weber, R. (1992). On the Gittins index for multiarmed bandits. *Annals of Applied Probability.*

Weick, K. E. (1995). *Sensemaking in organizations (Foundations for organizational science).* SAGE Publications, Inc.

West, G. (2017). *Scale: The universal laws life and death in organisms, cities and companies.* Penguin Press.

Yarbus, A. L. (1967). *Eye movements and vision.* Plenum Press.

Zuboff, S. (2019). *The age of surveillance capitalism: The fight for a human future at the new frontier of power.* PublicAffairs.

ABOUT THE AUTHOR

Ivo Velitchkov is a management consultant and enterprise architect. For the last 25 years, he has worked with big public and private organizations helping them with their strategy, structures and information. He has worked as a project manager, CEO, coach, consultant, researcher, and trainer. In all these roles he kept searching for the deeper principles that support organisms, organizations and society to live, survive, and thrive. Ivo has a PhD in Computer Science. He lives in Belgium with his wife and two children. He enjoys jazz concerts, playing tennis, sailing, and grooving the bass in a dad-rock cover band.

FIND OUT MORE

Find information about the eBook, the audio book, and the Essential Balances workshop at EssentialBalances.com

Read Ivo's blog: StrategicStructures.com

Follow Ivo on Twitter: twitter.com/kvistgaard

Connect on LinkedIn: linkedin.com/in/velitchkov

Printed in Great Britain
by Amazon

22062926R00156